Defining and Deploying Software Processes

Other Auerbach Publications in Software Development, Software Engineering, and Project Management

Defining and Deploying Software Processes

F. Alan Goodman

 Auerbach Publications
Taylor & Francis Group
Boca Raton New York

Published in 2006 by
Auerbach Publications
Taylor & Francis Group
6000 Broken Sound Parkway NW, Suite 300
Boca Raton, FL 33487-2742

International Standard Book Number-10: 0-8493-9845-2 (Hardcover)
International Standard Book Number-13: 978-0-8493-9845-2 (Hardcover)
Library of Congress Card Number 2005045280

Library of Congress Cataloging-in-Publication Data

Goodman, F. Alan.
   Defining and deploying software processes / F. Alan Goodman.
      p. cm.
   Includes index.
   ISBN 0-8493-9845-2
   1. Computer software--Development. I. Title.

QA76.76.D47G653 2005
005.1--dc22   2005045280

Taylor & Francis Group
is the Academic Division of T&F Informa plc.

Visit the Taylor & Francis Web site at
http://www.taylorandfrancis.com

and the Auerbach Publications Web site at
http://www.auerbach-publications.com

Contents

SECTION IV: DEPLOYING THE SOFTWARE PROCESS MODEL

List of Figures and Table

Figures

Table

Preface

For a long time, many people have urged me to write this book. Managers and practitioners from four companies encouraged me to do this.

I really want to help software management personnel who know that they need processes but have no idea how to go about creating them. My objectives are to define a process architecture that makes sense, connect it directly to real-world project tasking, provide implementation guidance, talk about all the ways that you really get real-world use out of it for your business, and, lastly, discuss how to deploy it in your company culture. I want this to be an "easy read" — not an academia-oriented book. You don't need a computer science modeling background to read this. You do need the will and desire to make process work for your organization. If you want to create a process bureaucracy just for that reason, you won't like this book.

I have seen companies rush into creating process "stuff" with no rhyme or reason to any architecture and end up with a pile of unusable (and expensive) garbage. If you recognize this situation, it's no wonder that process gets a bad name! On the other hand, if you follow my lead on developing process, it will open up all kinds of benefits, from people in the trenches to any company's bottom line and survivability in our global economy. You can get measurable improvements with this model.

This book will definitely help implementation for those of you addressing SPEM (Software Process Engineering Meta-model). SPEM has a voluminous specification to understand and this specification is written as most specifications are written: for technical readers. Whereas SPEM focuses on modeling processes, my book gets into process definition, implementation, usage, and deployment that can augment the SPEM models to make this real. You don't need UML (Universal Modeling Language) training and background to read my book. I use a single UML modeling diagram — the activity diagram. You will find out that it is central to defining the repeatable tasking world that shows up in process and in project schedules.

I kept putting off writing this book from 1991 until now. Over that period, I saw my wife's health worsen because of Parkinson's disease until deep brain surgery stabilized her condition significantly. Her deteriorating condition consumed me and affected my life drastically. I really feel that I could not have done justice to this book during those trying times. I realize now that if I do nothing in two years I'll only be two years older. If I tackle this book, I can be a published author and be two years older.

I am absolutely passionate about process. People who know me tell me that that passion shows! That same passion can cause potential employment issues when you're trying to change company cultures and may be perceived as a threat to entrenched managers. I believe as strongly in this presented method today as I did when I first developed this process architectural approach. I believe that any company that adopts this methodology will achieve dramatic process improvements that will show up as reduced time to market, reduced development costs, increased repeatability, improved quality, improved employee job satisfaction, improved customer satisfaction, and an overall better working environment throughout the entire company.

I've often thought that the term "process improvement" is incorrect because process is only one part (although an important part) of a more comprehensive term: "operations efficiency." If you can streamline business operations to be more cost-effective, shorten time to market, achieve repeatability, improve internal and external product quality, and increase profitability, process improvement is merely one main way to get there.

I will discuss aspects of this software process method over and over again from different perspectives. This method is very powerful and needs such repetition to cement in these important concepts. So, for those of you who are looking for real down-to-earth guidance in defining and implementing processes, this book is for you.

Acknowledgments

I am indebted to several people who have, in one way or another, directly or indirectly contributed to this book. I would like to thank Don Murphy who introduced me to the 7 M (Management) Tools. Of these, I adapted two of them (infinity brainstorming and interrelationship digraphs) in implementing this process approach. We had spirited process-related sessions over countless hours. I was fortunate to work with Jeff Herbert (software director at one company) who was (and is) an incredible human being and manager. Jeff always allowed me breathing space to talk about processes. He was willing to take up the cause to upper management when needed. It was Jeff who constantly reminded me that in the process development world we are playing horseshoes, not golf. His point was that to be close counts. For that, I thank him. I also thank Theresa Clowes for being a consummate editor and a real "process person" as a manager. There were times when I felt it was Theresa and me against the world. She was "with me" a lot in her understanding of this process methodology. I felt fortunate to work with and for this intelligent lady. While at a commercial company, I had the opportunity to have Karla Nolan work for me. We were an incredible team for process development. Karla partially implemented one version of this process framework for me on the company's intranet and was my ardent supporter. I also wish to thank Jim Vander Plaats whom I worked with (and for) at three different companies and who supported my process approach throughout all the periods of my employment. I would be remiss if I didn't thank Chris Holl and Dave Clinard of the San Diego chapter of the Society of Software Quality (SSQ), who provided me with a forum to expound on my process methodology at this professional society. I also want to thank John Barker, who really understood the relationship of good processes to achieving quality. While at a wireless telecommunication company in San Diego, I worked for Jim Thayer (head of the Base Station Controller), who provided an incredible level of support and understanding for what I was doing in the process area. With Jim's total support, I was able to accomplish much. As a process guy, you simply cannot succeed without that top-level support. I truly recognize these people because this book would not have been possible without their support.

In addition, both my adult sons, Darin and Scott Goodman, have encouraged me to go for it when I told them of my desire to write this book. They're proud of their old man.

I dedicate this book to my wife, Corinne. The debilitating progression of her Parkinson's disease has taken away any joy in this endeavor. I love her dearly and I am thankful for the years we have shared when she had good health. Lastly, I am enjoying being Grandpa to Chelsea and Anna Corinne Goodman. They are the two daughters I never had. I have an incredible new life viewpoint through these girls. Chelsea (now 14 years old) thinks it's real cool for Grandpa to write a book. I certainly can't let this important lady in my life down, eh?

Introduction

Background for This Book

I gravitated into the process world several years ago after performing almost all roles in the software engineering environment — both as a programmer and in various management positions. That environment covered both the commercial software development world and the government contracting software development world. I kept getting back to a process focus after personally witnessing complete disasters with so-called process-rich environments and alternatively process-sparse environments. I often ran into "process people" who lost sight of the fact that processes were there to support the organization — not the other way around! Frustrations at all levels have been enormous for software engineering personnel.

I was in the trenches and in software management during the U.S. government's push for making Department of Defense (DoD) software contractors conform to standards like MIL-Std-1679, DoD-Std-2167, and, later, DoD-Std-2167A. The government's zeal in getting pesky contractors in line during that period resulted in vast documentation standards requirements throughout the development life cycle — even when those deliverables were illogical at various times in the life cycle. Companies were unsuccessfully trying to force a real-world development life cycle onto a waterfall-based model from the government. The government openly advocated tailoring the imposed model, but when you did just that, government employees suspected you of trying to get away with something, and thus effective tailoring was not done. I was there and I know what really went on to try to conform. The government related document production to project progress regardless of document quality. Repeatability translated into creating a standard set of documents with standard formats. Software contractors ended up in the document business rather than the software business to a large extent. The government alleged to just describe "what" had to be done but the same government had all kinds of "how-tos" included as well — including defining low-level document formats via Data Item Descriptions (DIDs) for just about everything. Woe betide anyone who deviated from any government DID — even if it made sense! The cost of government-imposed "process" was enormous with questionable value, in my opinion.

After this fiasco, add in all the variations of what gurus said you had to have in order to be good at processes. These included the Software Capability Model (SW-CMM), the System Engineering Capability Model (SE-CMM), personal/team/acquisition models, and, later, the integrated version of software/systems — the CMMI (Capability Maturity Model — Integrated). The CMMI added an additional decision point of staged versus continuous representations (over four model variations each) to provide a forward path from the legacy software or systems capability maturity model. When you throw in things like ISO 9001, ISO 9000-3, TickIT, Malcolm Baldrige awards, Six Sigma, etc., it's no wonder that the average person views process with jaundiced eyes and considers the next thing down the line as yet another "flavor of the month." In the rush to get with this program or that program, companies had lost sight of the very reason that we need better processes! Good processes save time and money, reduce life-cycle costs, reduce time to market, increase repeatability, increase quality, improve competitiveness, and improve employee and customer satisfaction — if done right! I've added that caveat because I have seen horrible examples of processes that have succeeded in achieving the opposite goal.

I wish to point out that no maturity model or standard addresses how process elements are organized (process framework architecture) or how they are accessible for real-world usage. They also don't address how to implement processes, value-added aspects, and deployment issues. This is where this book fits in. This is a great adjunct book to developing those CMMI/ISO-based processes so that all the pieces fit into the giant jigsaw puzzle in an organized and modular fashion. Without clean process architecture, you can end up with piles and piles of process "stuff" that becomes useless real fast and is less and less maintainable. I have seen that very condition. When companies get to that state, they may have processes, but they really don't because you end up with process variations, different process versions, and process inconsistencies. You get to play the "which one do I believe" game or "which one is right" game. If you are in this state, you need this book. If you are going to tackle CMMI or ISO 9001 and don't have processes, you need this book. My role is as a process architect. My role is not being a domain-knowledgeable individual for the way you do business. Because of this separation, I can apply this architectural model to any kind of business or any kind of governmental entity. I have been involved already with hospital systems. Even my eye doctor has recognized that he has a life cycle with process elements to run his office. This supports my assumption that there are domain people out there who can apply this architectural model to their specific business or governmental system. For that reason, I go into a company as a process architect, not as a domain expert in all types of business. It would be vain of me to consider taking that approach (and it would be disastrous to even think about it).

Being an internal CMM assessor and an internal ISO auditor, I have encountered volumes of manual documents in people's offices that are purported to be processes. The sheer weight of these manuals tends to discourage most people. I've even seen these artifacts with their plastic wrap still on or with pristine pages; this has left me with the sense that they have not even been looked at. The intranet can have a large process repository, but allow usage to be focused on the part you really want — usually on a single Web page! Notice the similarity to Web surfing, where you get the information you want quickly. Paper, however, just sits there in your bookcase. If I were to hand you one or more volumes of paper-based processes, you would gulp and set it aside immediately. If I could get you to what you were interested in — in three clicks (or less) — and present you with a single Web page, you would be more likely to follow it. If I provided you with a short list of standard process element types, you would understand and use them.

Process is not unlike a résumé. You write a résumé on the assumption that you have, at best, 30 seconds of time to grab the reader's attention. If you don't, it gets discarded. Process has an even tighter time window. If users cannot get to what they want in three clicks (or less), they get frustrated and essentially discard it. This book is very conscious and aware of this phenomenon for process success. My point is that you could have the greatest process content in the world, but if you can't get to it efficiently, you lose. Conversely, you lose if you can get to process elements efficiently but once there the content is crappy. You need both elements in play for success. I deal with both of these worlds in this book.

It always amazed me that processes, even if they existed, were either totally ignored, treated with disdain, or forced down people's throats. I have even been in companies where the word "process" couldn't even be spelled! One company thought that process meant only having some forms. Another company considered process as only some templates! Yet another company thought that process meant writing piles of stuff in the hope that somebody finds something that he or she can use! We have a problem when we can't even define what this thing is and yet without it, companies can fail and go bankrupt. Even for struggling companies, employers can lose money while employees get ulcers and become stressed, due to workplace chaos.

Just watch the daily TV news if you want to see how badly the government deals with process! The government routinely mixes and matches what you have to do with a one-size-fits-all mentality for how-tos. I cringe when I hear U.S. senators and representatives misuse process terms. I must admit, I've seen some attempts at the what/how separation that are usually targeted at complex regulations that shouldn't be that way in the first place. A classic example is the IRS! The IRS tax rules and regulations are so complicated that you can't get consistent answers from people within the IRS for the same question! The federal, state, and county governments wonder why businesses go under when they stuff government regulations down a company's throat and treat a 5-person company like a 5,000-person company! You would think that the government would actually want to set up the environment for small businesses to exist and grow — thus hiring people and contributing to the tax base. When small business has to hire people just to deal with government regulations (the same regulation as that 5,000-person company deals with), something is wrong! These are process problems.

How many TV events and major issues are process-related? Try Middle East issues, prisoner detainment issues, Iraq and Afghanistan transition issues, stock transactions, troop training issues, 9/11 responses, mad cow disease, wildfires, gasoline distribution and pricing, school district issues, homeland security threat levels... Process is at the heart of all these major issues. One manager told me that I totally destroyed his TV news viewing because he saw process problems in just about everything he watched, just like I did.

When politicians get involved with these monumental events and issues, they say they are going to address process but invariably use commissions and special bodies to be in the political partisan business — not process solutions. You see political bashing or political supporting based on party affiliations with no real attention to things like "what went wrong?" or "how can we do better?" types of process focus. I have often thought that if the 9/11 Commission had been staffed with process people, the outcome would have been significantly different. The focus would have been on process, roles, what was done or should be done, resource management and allocation, training, etc. Process people are not in the blame business at all, whereas politicians are in the blame business. Process people know that blame is death to improving processes. Politicians use blame to enhance themselves or deflect attention away from themselves for votes.

Most governments are poor at process as most legislators are not "process people." Our government does not separate what you need to do from how you need to do it, especially when it comes to regulating business. I can't tell you how many people I've talked to in our hospitals that complain a lot about FDA regulations mixing "whats" and "hows" at a high cost within those hospitals. At the how-to level, the government does a poor job of process tailoring through alternative selections. This lack of scalable solutions contributes to high costs, high overhead, unnecessary complexity, and low compliance. This alone causes many businesses to go under unnecessarily.

I have personally experienced incredible complexity in hiring a caregiver for my wife just to comply with state and federal employer rules! I get treated like a huge corporation rather than an individual. Equal opportunity posters were sent to me for posting (along with warnings) when I hired the caregiver. Do I tape these posters behind the toilet to comply? My point here is that overbearing processes imposed by governmental entities range from bizarre to oppressive. It's no wonder there's a thriving underground economy that bypasses government processes! The state and federal government only have themselves to blame for this state of affairs. These are government process problems.

As a new Medicare recipient, have you tried reading the government literature on this? I consider myself a fairly intelligent person but after reading and rereading government materials, it's almost like they have an underlying motive of making things as complicated as possible. You read terms like "Medigap" and "Medicare plus Choice" in government literature with an "or" between them with no explanation supporting this "or." It took me several phone calls to understand this difference. My point here is that the government does a poor job of separating "what" from "how." Also, the "how" part needs to have variations clearly spelled out so that there is no single one-size-fits-all "how" described. I challenge anyone out there to look at government documents from a process perspective for complete understandability. You won't get it.

The process approach basics described in this book could revolutionize government at all layers and actually cause businesses to thrive and succeed at the same time! I urge government personnel at all levels to consciously separate "what you have to do" from "how you are to do it." Government regulations should exist at the "what" level with high-level requirements. The government needs to recognize business scaling and provide alternative how-to suggestions if they feel they need to be in the how-to business. Never mix the "what" level and the "how" level. With this separation, government could then provide a scalable set of "how-tos" if they really wanted to provide guidance for differing-sized classes of customers. A 5-person company would be treated more reasonably for a small company rather than forcing it to behave like a 5,000-person company. The small company could actually hire more people to contribute to the tax base rather than hiring people just to support government overhead. What a concept!

The government is notorious for addressing problems where the cost of solution is way out of proportion to the relativity of the problem. In business, you want to use Pareto charts to tackle the big things first, to get the biggest bang for the buck. As a process guy, I am well aware of this focus point. In government, however, you may work on the 2 percent items first because of various factors that have no basis in process. The "pain" selection may be purely political with no rational basis for selection. Can you imagine what the government would be like if spending was based on process metrics? That is, you don't get massive funding for the little stuff first. The taxpayer dollars would be far better spent based on some measurable basis of need — not special interest pressures.

It has been my experience that commercial companies will get serious with process when they're up against the wall and have to deal with survivability from competition. Many U.S. companies will need to work smarter to survive in a global economy. Government contractors get with process because the government makes them (and for the company to "stay in the game"). Ironically, process people tend to be the first to be laid off when things get tough — even though they could be the very people who can be instrumental in turning a company around. Additionally, process people can be viewed as "making waves" or even as "trouble-makers" when trying to get needed changes made in an organization. During those tough times, executives go right to the "cutting heads" solution and tend not to consider the process world as another huge savings opportunity at all. Amazing! Process specialists are not that different from emergency room doctors. If you can get to the patient in time, you can save the patient — if not, the patient dies. For process specialists, that patient is the company. Companies can get real sick and die — just like people. We all know of companies that used to exist that are no longer around.

In all the process-based environments described above, you end up with practitioners and managers who develop very negative opinions about processes. It could be a nasty four-letter word to many people. If you hear things like "What turkey dreamed this up?" in describing process elements, you'll have an awful time introducing any new (and what is perceived to be the next "flavor") processes. I know because I have walked into environments just like that.

Add to all of this a potpourri of process terms that are inconsistent, inaccurate, and wrong. It's no wonder that the average person is totally confused and irritated by this process stuff. Stay tuned — I hope to change your opinion about the incredible value of doing process right.

Purpose of This Book

With all this foundational background, I am going to turn my attention to the very essence of this book. In all my years in the process world having to deal with standards and maturity models, they focus on endgame requirements (or perceived requirements) and don't deal with process architectural structures, presentation, usefulness, deployment, or people aspects of process. The toughest aspect of defining and implementing process is the people part. People resist change — even good change. Some people will smile at you while stabbing you in the back behind the scenes over process. I have experienced that personally and have added a section of this book that will mitigate some of this.

I have consciously written this book from a lay perspective for a broad reader base. If you really want to create processes in an organized fashion that are absolutely useful and tie the process world to your project schedules, you need this book. My objective was to provide guidance for that definition and implementation of your processes. I also wanted to show you why you get enormous value from this approach in running your business. Lastly, I wanted to provide guidance on how to deploy processes into your company culture. This is the toughest part of all. You will end up with a Web-based process architecture that is completely flexible and extensible where you need it. You will also end up with a process approach that will be embraced by your employees because it is sensible.

This book will address these four major sections:

- Definition of the software process architectural model. This is the jigsaw puzzle that describes what the pieces and parts are and how they fit together in a cohesive way.
- Implementation of the software process architectural model. This addresses the importance of the Web to access process along with the importance of a version-controlled repository tool for process management. I provide implementation guidance to build the process pieces and parts such that they fit into this jigsaw puzzle.
- Using the software process model. This section addresses the following topics:
  - Classes of process users
  - Metrics collection and presentation
  - Schedule creation and management including earned value
  - Project estimation
  - Time-card charging
  - Subcontract management
  - Integrated teaming

- Deploying this software process model into an organization. This involves the following issues:
  - Getting at pain issues rapidly
  - Process group creation and charter
  - Process champion development (domino theory)
  - Piloting the software process model
  - Measuring the software process model
  - Preparing for an external model appraisal (like Standard CMMI Appraisal Method for Process Improvement [SCAMPI])

All are important for process success. The first two bullets deal with process structure and implementation of that structure. The third bullet deals with how to use this software process method within your organization for those real benefits. The last bullet involves making sure that this method stays in your organization and becomes part of your process culture.

If I had a "wrapper" term for this software process model, it would be called Selectable Process Architecture, or SPA. The heart and soul of this SPA is the ability to pick and choose process elements at all levels while balancing mandated repeatable elements with nonmandated procedural elements. As you progress through this book, this process balance will become more evident to you. Because of this built-in selectability, this model is completely extensible for real-world process adaptability. This software process model allows you to completely change your process basis over time in an orderly fashion — discarding what doesn't work while retaining what does work. Over the years, I've hated it when I'm told things like "that's just the way it is" when describing process. With this approach you are not stuck with archaic or nonsense solutions. With this approach you can also expand tool support naturally.

THE SOFTWARE PROCESS MODEL

Chapter 1

Origins of the Software Process Model

Many years ago, I visited a large aerospace company complex in the eastern United States. While there, I was introduced to their engineering processes. They had many, many manuals of processes that were color coded by functional area usage. This was their approach to functional area separation. In the software volumes, they did one thing that was an absolute revelation to me — they consciously separated "what you need to do" from "how you need to do it." It was such a fundamental concept and yet it has not been done by many companies, even today! That inspired the idea for this process framework architecture. You need to consciously separate "what you do" from "how you do it." The way they approached the "what" level, however, was immersed in the Department of Defense (DoD) 2167 standard of that day for terminology and document deliverables. They only addressed what you had to do at high-level 2167 phases as described in that standard. The granularity of their "whats" was at a real high level for the software engineering phase level. Their process implementation paralleled the standard for phases and expected deliverables within each phase. This means that their implementation was a document-centric view of the "what you have to do" world. Their "how-to" world" was a pile of process stuff (in how-to process element number order) that was just "there." You could not pull out a how-to process element from the pile and get an answer to the question, "Where does this fit?" I felt that this was a huge mistake. It became a requirement in this proposed software process architecture that process elements had to fit somewhere and that one should be able to answer that "where does it fit" question. My impression was that this process mapping to the DoD 2167 standard did wonders for the government auditors and company management but did little for the people actually doing the work — the practitioners.

Because their process implementation was based at the phase level, it separated the entire process world from the real world. What I mean by that is that actual work to be done was shown on project schedules. These "what you need to do" elements, when rolled up on a schedule, become summary lines or phases. Their implementation only addressed phase-based items or, in scheduling parlance, the summary line. There was no connection to the task level of a schedule where real work is mapped out. I determined this to be a problem and wanted to correct that process/schedule connection to the lower granularity of the schedule task. Let's face it — the task is where the action is for process repeatability.

"Phases" in the real world are, at best, umbrella terms for a particular set of schedule tasks. A traditional phase name is like a summary roll-up term on a schedule. For the most part, actual tasks within each phase were however anyone wanted to describe them. Task descriptions were all over the place. Some were noun-based, some verb-based, and both had huge variations related to levels of detail. Schedule tasks had no connection to the process stuff on this earlier software process model. You hoped that the actual day-to-day work made a "hit" with some of the process items described in these traditional phase-based process manuals. How all this happened on a day-to-day basis was that programmers would march through the software life cycle working tasks and periodically hope that something out there in the process world would help them. You could not take randomly selected schedule tasks and connect them to discrete process items. It was this disconnect from the real world that I also thought was a huge mistake. This also became a cornerstone of my process architecture. The "whats" had to directly relate to the real world of schedules. This meant that the granularity of each "what you had to do" had to exactly map to schedule tasking. This was a huge difference from their approach.

For this large company, the how-to process elements were placed in a big pile of stuff. You could not relate any of these process elements to a schedule task nor could you relate any of these process elements with events or stimuli. You could not determine where something fit. The "fit" selection was a hit-and-miss kind of thing based on a key word or phrase. If you were doing an inspection or evaluation, was there something out there that was called "evaluation" or "inspection" that might be useful to you? If you picked the right word or term, you'd get a "hit" — if not, you wouldn't. In this software process architecture, each and every how-to process element had to exist for a reason and had to be tied to asynchronous events or stimuli or be tied to high-level steps within a scheduled activity (task).

After looking at their phase-based processes and unconnected how-to procedure piles, it became obvious to me that there should be clear-cut mapping of both to real-world actions. Having said that, the real world to me is as follows:

■ The set of tasks to be done in a project schedule. These are the "what you have to do" process elements that address connected actions based on stimuli/responses to or from other schedule tasks. Schedule tasks are connected in the real world of actual work to be done (i.e., you can't do the successor task unless the predecessor task is done). Another way of stating this is that the output from one task becomes the input to another task. Also, each schedule task should be treated as an uninterruptible element. These tasks (or activities) contain the high-level steps that may (or may not) have how-to elaborations. An implementation activity is done after a low-level design activity and both can be placed on a project schedule showing that predecessor/successor relationship. These are schedulable process elements because they can be shown on a project schedule.

■ The set of how-to process elements that have "scope." The scope of any how-to can be summarized as follows:

  – A how-to process element can be an elaboration of one or more high-level "what" steps within a schedulable activity or task. These how-to process elements are connected to the schedulable world of processes. An example of this how-to would be the "end" procedure that is connected to the "end" high-level step in each schedulable activity to notify activity termination and pass off activity metrics.

  – A how-to process element can be an asynchronous event (i.e., not schedulable) and can have a scope of a single phase in the project life cycle. These how-to process elements are not connected to the schedulable world of processes and are considered event-driven how-tos. These are how-to procedures that are different based on which phase they get executed in. This is the situation where a coding phase how-to is different from an integration phase how-to for the same kind of how-to.

  – A how-to process element can be an asynchronous event (i.e., not schedulable) and can have a scope of a single segment (a collection of phases) in the project life cycle. These how-to process elements are not connected to the schedulable world of processes and are considered event-driven how-tos. An example of this might be a requirements change procedure that is different in the pre-execution (prior to project turn-on) segment than it is in the execution segment (after project turn-on).

– A how-to process element can be an asynchronous event (i.e., not schedulable) and can have effectively no scope. These how-to process elements are not connected to the schedulable world of processes and are considered event-driven how-tos that are independent of phases or segments. An example of this might be a quality-related corrective action how-to that is identical no matter what phase or segment you are in.

In this same institution, I could take phase-based process elements and clearly tie them to some phase in the life cycle. I could not tie actual tasking elements that showed up on a schedule to anything within that phase-based process element. This "what you have to do" level was merely wording that collected dust. Their procedures were worse. I had no idea where these fit in any life cycle or how they were connected within any phase of that life cycle. In addition, they had different flavors of the same procedure out there. Which one do you pick? Also, it appeared to me that if you felt like writing a procedure, you just did! It became another requirement in my software process model that all process elements have to have some reason for being. Also, in my approach, if you feel like writing a how-to, where's the "what" that it's connected to? The how-to reasons for being break down into five fundamental categories:

■ To elaborate on a high-level "what" step within an activity
■ To satisfy a high-level "what" requirement (e.g., to satisfy an ISO 9001 standard requirement)
■ To satisfy a high-level "what" perceived requirement (e.g., to satisfy a CMMI process maturity goal/standard practice)
■ To satisfy implied industry best practices
■ To satisfy some kind of stimulus

I did not include the need to satisfy the "process" person! I say this because some process people seem to have the need to wallpaper the walls with everything that moves. I am not advocating that at all. In fact, not all things need process elements. We need to be sensible about this. Keep in mind that process exists to support the organization, not the other way around. I am not interested in creating a process bureaucracy just for the sake of it.

Another area of contention that I saw was in the compliance area. There was no mapping of how-to procedural elements to anything. At the phase-based process level, the best you could say was that one phase equaled one DoD 2167 phase — as specified in this government standard. The concept of mapping process elements to any standard or maturity model was nonexistent. It became vital in this model to make sure that you had complete traceability to these high-level requirements. High-level process requirements external to your processes include such things as company policies, government regulations, and international standards (e.g., ISO 9001:2000). High-level perceived requirements include maturity models like CMMI goals/process areas/practices and SW-CMM. Process elements traced to these can be both activities (what you need to do) and procedures (how you need to do it). High-level "whats" internal to your processes include the high-level "what" steps within any schedulable activity. Process elements traced to these high-level "what" steps are strictly how-to procedures.

In addition to explicit requirements, I recognized that process elements and ordering of those elements are also based on the type of business you have. It was important in this model to recognize the existence of process elements that satisfy implied requirements as well. Both activities and procedures can exist to satisfy an implied industry best practice. For example, a software engineering company knows that something needs to be coded before you test it. You need process activities that relate to these schedulable tasks and show these predecessor/successor relationships.

The earlier "what" level processes and procedures failed to communicate the driver or stimulus that caused them to be executed. For the phase-based processes, the only stimulus was that a phase was declared so we must be in that phase's processes. I could not clearly identify the inputs/outputs that provided the thread of actions at all. It became important that activities at the "what" level have clear drivers for execution. Similarly, procedures have clear anchors for execution. Just as schedule tasks are stimulus-driven as predecessor/successor tasks on a schedule, process activities are similar and can also be mapped onto a schedule. In the schedulable world, it is the process activity that is invoked as a result of a stimulus. Procedures can also be stimulus-driven. If something happens, invoke a specific procedure.

One company where I worked (as well as the company mentioned at the beginning of this chapter) felt that "tailoring" (especially at the how-to level) involved writing all-inclusive process descriptions and physically redlining out any excesses to make it more appropriate for smaller efforts. This approach created a "one-size-fits-all" mentality for how-to process element creation that targeted the largest possible scope of effort. When people tailored these process elements for smaller efforts, it was time-consuming and error-prone, and the end result was useless as a process to be followed. This tailoring approach became another cornerstone of my approach. It became important that you mandate the "whats" but have both flexibility and extensibility at the "how" level. Tailoring is to be done by providing alternative selections (one aspect of the software process model method) — not by redlining a single one-size-fits-all how-to process element. If you're in the process arena long enough, you realize that the biggest arguments deal with how things are done. There are very few arguments related to what needs to be done — particularly in an engineering development environment. If you allow (and encourage) different how-tos as part of your model, you get rid of most process-related arguments! Another phenomenon happens over time: winning how-to procedures survive and losing how-to procedures die naturally as part of normal process improvement.

It is important to point out that many seed ideas in this process model came out of my earlier experiences. For the first time, I clearly determined what was wrong and what was right with what I saw.

I then embarked on preaching about this new approach both internally via company lunchtime sessions, at company engineering forums, at local San Diego Society for Software Quality (SSQ) chapter meetings, and by speaking at the Software Engineering Process Group (SEPG) conference in Atlantic City, New Jersey. My message regarding this new approach has been totally consistent during all this time.

What I Will Cover

Given my personal experiences on both sides of the process fence and seeing what worked and what didn't work, I formed a process architecture framework model that is both simple and yet profound on many levels to really address a total software process solution to any company. I wanted to provide a software process model that was rich enough to fully address Design for Six Sigma (DFSS), the eight versions of CMMI across two representations, and ISO 9001 certification with a simple practitioner directive of "just follow the process!" without anyone really knowing CMMI, ISO, Six Sigma, Malcolm Baldrige, or anything else. This process model achieves just that.

I realized very early that process has several classes of "customers." Process customers break down to direct customers and indirect customers (beneficiaries). Each customer class has to be satisfied (what's in it for me?). The process approach needed to completely satisfy all classes of customers from the executives down to the people in the trenches (prac-

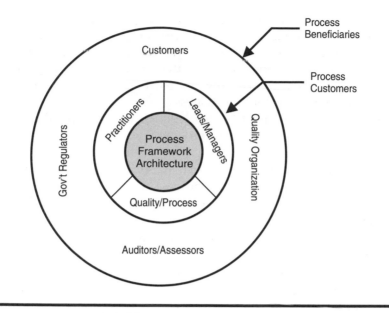

Process Beneficiaries

Process Customers

Customers

Practitioners

Leads/Managers

Process Framework Architecture

Gov't Regulators

Quality Organization

Quality/Process

Auditors/Assessors

Figure 1.1 Process stakeholders.

titioners). If you satisfy one group to the detriment of another group, you lose. I've seen this in real life when you have marvelous, pretty, and colorful high-level process graphics to satisfy executives but these graphics are absolutely useless to the very people who need to follow them — the practitioners.

I also realized that process success had as much to do with process organization and accessibility as it had to do with process content. The point here is that if it's not fast and convenient for access, it doesn't matter what the actual process target is — because people will not use it. Conversely, an efficient framework architecture tied to easy access facilitates institutionalization of processes.

Figure 1.1 depicts the classes of people who directly interface with the core processes. These are the primary process customers. In addition to these classes of people, there are others who are direct beneficiaries of that core process as well. These are considered secondary process customers. The combined set of people comprise all the stakeholders of process. In one way or another, they are all affected by process.

Coming into an organization with a process framework architecture in mind is not enough to make it successful. You need to have that process model architecture "in your back pocket" and attack the company pain issues or certification issues as your external thrust. If you solve the organization's problems and frustrations or department issues, that's what is considered a success. As an aside in addressing these pain issues, you implement the process framework architecture! Organizations do not take kindly to anyone coming in with any real or perceived magic bullet to process organization or structure. I happen to believe strongly that I have that magic bullet but I don't advertise that. As a "process guy," I had to constantly fight managers who just wanted to add things to the process pile with no thought to their usefulness.

Over the last few years, it became very clear to me that five elements have to be in place to succeed in process:

- You need an overall process framework architectural approach into which you implement your process solutions (back-pocket item). This part addresses the process framework into which process pieces or parts fit.
- You need to identify the company "pain" issues and tie process progress to those pain issues. These become the process drivers for the process framework architecture.
- You need a process environment for success. This includes management support and a commitment to addressing the process drivers.
- You need a Web solution that specifically addresses usability and access to the process world.
- You need a version-controlled process repository to maintain multiple versions and to provide a rapid change process.

From an ordering perspective, these three main ingredients look like Figure 1.2.

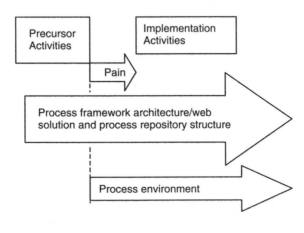

Figure 1.2 Process ingredient ordering.

I will cover how I have approached process framework architecture deployment into an organization without the organization truly realizing that this was the main event. The organization thought that I was only solving their process pain issues whereas I was really addressing these stakeholders:

- The practitioners want something useful: something that will work for them on a day-by-day basis and something that frees them from all the extraneous stuff beyond the very reason they were hired. Average software programmers view this process stuff as the BS aspect of their work.
- The management wants to see better quality, fewer costs, reduced time to market, better repeatability, and improved customer product satisfaction.
- The executives want to feel that we really have a handle on all this. They want high-level pretty graphics to show prospective customers how good we are at addressing processes or how we get certified.
- The customers want to feel good about our ability to perform as a consistent quality supplier.
- The quality management wants compliance to stated company quality goals — i.e., CMMI, Six Sigma process foundation, ISO 9001, etc.
- The quality engineers want a process methodology that is truly auditable. Engineering is also interested in doing self-quality checks in the true spirit of ISO 9001's definition of "quality" without a quality organization.
- The internal and external assessors want to see a comprehensive approach to process that shows process compliance and a process basis that is truly institutionalized.

I hope to show why this presented approach provides you with an incredible solution to a plethora of company process problems. I also hope to show government management and elected officials why the basics of this approach directly provide a business-friendly solution to government regulators.

In dealing with this topic, I have a chicken-and-egg issue. I need to talk about the software process framework architecture first, yet the real thrust is getting business pain issues inserted into that framework. In addition, in discussing the main process architecture focus, I need to quantify what the real world means. When discussing the process framework, I need to touch on implementation and deployment topics. When

I discuss the implementation and deployment topics, I need to talk about the process framework architecture. I hope you will bear with me about this dilemma.

Process Terminology

Before giving an overview of this process framework model, it is important at this point to be very specific about the process terminology that I use in describing the details of this process framework architecture.

I have heard it all for process terms. I have been amazed at what people use throughout the industry for process terms — some terms are incredibly bad. How many of you have heard the phrase "policies and procedures" on the network news (usually after process disasters)? This term is used as if it related to one thing — but it's really two entirely separate topics! Policies should be high-level assertive statements whereas procedures should be implementation how-tos! In this process model, the former is at the "authority" level whereas the latter is at the "implementation" level — these are separated by the "repeatability" level. Some think work instructions are almost anything but that term is appropriate for very low-level instructions that you might find in a manufacturing environment. Some think "procedures" means almost anything whereas that term is more appropriate for how-tos that can range from high-level through low-level descriptions. Some use both terms where it is real fuzzy why something is called one thing versus the other. In this model, I encourage a high-level how-to (procedure) that may or may not have a low-level elaboration counterpart (work instruction). This is to accommodate the experienced user from the novice. It will be obvious why you make that distinction if you're an experienced user that's irritated by too much detail. I've seen so-called policies that contain what you should do, how to do it, and that include company titles to do things. How's that for creating something that is guaranteed to be wrong over time! I've also seen ISO-certified companies where company policies essentially replicate ISO 9001 requirements. In this last case, you have to question why the company policy exists.

Given that backdrop, I am proposing the following terms that have discrete meanings and have discrete places within the process framework architecture where they reside. I realize that each company has built-in cultures and built-in usage of terms that may not exactly agree with my terms. In those instances, relate your terms with mine. I also realize that you may need to revisit these terms as you get into the meat of the process framework architecture. It is important that I be totally consistent with terms throughout this book for their semantics in the process repository and usage.

- Activity — A process element that corresponds to a schedule task containing a series of high-level "what" steps that you need to do. An instance of an activity becomes a schedule task. Some companies call these standard practices. This feature is an integral part of the software process model.
- Activity group — A logical group of activities used for process metrics purposes when executed on schedules. "Design" may be the set of activities involved in design whether at the system, subsystem, or component levels.
- Compliance matrix — A spreadsheet or database that maps requirements of the target compliance standard/model to process elements that address those requirements. Quality/process groups for standards compliance, maturity model compliance, or regulation compliance primarily use these artifacts.
- EDP lists (area) — Event-driven procedures lists area that is connected to each and every Process Activity Diagram (PAD), showing those how-to procedural elements that are stimulus- or event-driven versus those connected to high-level steps within each activity. These processes are nonschedulable.
- End-to-end life cycle — A pictorial view of activities showing predecessor/successor relationships between those activities. The end-to-end life cycle integrates roles at both the intra-activity and inter-activity levels to support concurrent engineering. An expanded "morphed" view of this becomes the project schedule showing activity instances (schedule tasks). The end-to-end life cycle is made up of horizontal PADs.
- Form examples — Completed forms that are suitable to be used as examples.
- Form guidelines — Optional and separate helpful hints to fill in a complex form. Guidelines can also be embedded in the form template as a visible aid or as a nonvisible aid ("hidden text").
- Form inspection checklist — The optional quality checklist associated with any particular (and usually complex) form. Most forms do not need a form inspection checklist.
- Form matrix — A spreadsheet or database mapping forms to process elements. This provides a form-centric view of the process model showing where forms are created and updated by process element.
- Form selector — An implementation that allows selection of forms for form tailoring. It is a feature that is an integral part of this

software process model and also provides the mechanism for flexibility and extensibility regarding forms. Used primarily on a Web-based implementation to map generic forms at the activity level to specific forms used at execution time.

■ Form set — Associated process elements for any form. These include the form template, optional form inspection checklist, optional form guidelines, and optional form examples.

■ Form template — The skeleton form that is used as a basis for filling in the form.

■ Functional description — A process element that describes all aspects of a functional topic in terms of pertinent process elements to that functional area. "Requirements management" is a functional area that has both activities and how-to elements that address that functional area.

■ Government regulations — Umbrella term for various governmental regulations to be followed in certain types of industries (e.g., FDA/FAA regulations). Government regulations are part of the "authority" level in this process model.

■ Government standards — Umbrella term for standards like MIL-Std-498, 2167A, 12207, etc. Can also include standards from other governmental agencies containing requirements to be followed. Government standards are part of the "authority" level in this process model.

■ How selector — An implementation that allows selection of how-to procedures and work instructions for how-to tailoring. A feature that is an integral part of this software process model. Also provides the mechanism for flexibility and extensibility for how-to process elements.

■ How-to process element — Umbrella term for a procedure or work product.

■ International standards — Umbrella term for standards like ISO 9001 that contain process requirements to be followed. International standards are part of the "authority" level in this process model.

■ Planning package — A term to describe a schedule plan or estimation of work to be done. As visibility gets better and better as a result of increasing design, planning packages are replaced with work packages that reflect what really needs to be done.

■ Policy — High-level, assertive, company-based process requirement. Policies should be short and unambiguous as to intent. These should not replicate other authority-level requirements like ISO 9001, government regulations, government standards, etc.

- Procedure — A how-to process element that elaborates on either a high-level step in an activity or a process requirement "what." A feature that is an integral part of this software process model. All procedures are to be associated with a particular how selector. A procedure can be a high-level how-to description, flowchart, or mind-jogger checklist. This model's Web implementation encourages a short procedure as a single Web page and an associated work instruction for those procedures where you want more verbose descriptions. This separation accommodates experienced users versus inexperienced users.
- Process activity diagram (PAD) — A subset pictorial representation of the end-to-end story. A small set of PADs, usually representing a project phase or major tollgate period and oriented to major functional areas to form the total end-to-end story. Each PAD is a single Web-page implementation oriented to major functional groups. This is a similar concept in Rational's Unified Modeling Language (UML) for activity diagrams but specific to process elements.
- Process element — Umbrella term for an activity, procedure, or work instruction.
- Response — The result of a stimulus. This is the major basis for this process approach. Process elements do not exist unless there is a transformation of a stimulus (input) to a response (output).
- Roles matrix — A spreadsheet or database mapping roles to process elements. This provides a role-centric view of the process model showing where roles are involved by process element.
- SPA — Selectable Process Architecture (method). A potential umbrella term for this particular process architecture that promotes selectability throughout the model for process efficiency and usefulness.
- Stimulus — The basis of a process action, which in turn causes a response. This is the major basis for this process approach. Process elements do not exist unless there is a transformation of a stimulus (input) to a response (output).
- Training matrix — A spreadsheet or database mapping training to process elements. This provides a training-centric view of the process model showing where training is involved by process element.
- Training package — Training for one or more process views. Training can be specific to a single process element or can be across process elements (vertically or horizontally).

■ Virtual document — A special wrapper-type of work product that is essentially an outer document wherein a table of contents points to other (and different) work products. The virtual document producer makes no attempt to copy information into a single document but produces a single top-level wrapper document that references the set of work products that comprise it.

■ Work breakdown structure (WBS) — A product-oriented, process-oriented indentured tree composed of efforts expended in a project. Project charges are based on the WBS breakdown. For this process model, there is a direct correlation from process activities, schedule tasking (instances of process activities), and time charging.

■ Work instruction — A low-level (or verbose) procedural how-to process element. A feature that is an integral part of this software process model. In this model's Web implementation, we encourage a top-level mind-jogger checklist or flowchart as a procedure with its elaborated counterpart as a work instruction. For those companies that only want verbose how-tos, they will probably only have work instructions and no procedures. Work instruction elaborations on any procedure are meant to satisfy the novice user.

■ Work package — A synonymous term for a scheduled task or an instance of a process activity. A work package is what gets executed on a schedule and is the basis for any earned value calculation.

■ Work product — Resultant product of executed activities that signifies "done" for any activity. A feature that is an integral part of this software process model. Work products are tangible artifacts for any response.

■ Work product examples — Real examples of completed work products. Examples are a marvelous way to improve production and reduce time to market.

■ Work product guidelines — Optional and separate helpful hints to creating any work product. Guidelines can also be embedded in the work product template.

■ Work product inspection checklist — The quality checklist associated with a particular work product. In this process model, this artifact also includes entry criteria (for author) and role-based criteria to aid in qualified inspector selection and focus.

■ Work product matrix — A spreadsheet or database mapping work products to process elements. This provides a work product-centric view of the process model showing where work products are created or updated by process elements.

■ Work product selector — An implementation that allows selection of work products for work product tailoring. A feature that is an integral part of this software process model. Also provides the mechanism for flexibility and extensibility for work products. Used primarily on a Web-based implementation to map generic work products at the activity level to specific work products used at execution time.

■ Work product set — Associated process elements for any work product. These include the work product template, work product inspection checklist, optional work product guidelines, and optional work product examples.

■ Work product template — The skeleton work product that is used as a basis for building the work product.

Chapter 2

Defining the Real-World Process Connection

The very essence of this book deals with connecting the world of processes to the real world of scheduling and life-cycle management. What is the "real world"? I have seen all kinds of company processes that are not connected to the real world. Many companies have piles of process stuff out there and they hope that something out there might be useful if someone remembers that a process element exists. If you have this situation, put on your seat belts because I will directly tie processes to the real world.

Initially, I considered the real world to be represented by the project schedule that really needs that process connection. After all, isn't the project schedule a true reflection of actual tasks to be done? A schedule task has these characteristics:

- It reflects work to be done (i.e., it is a set of actions).
- It reflects a transformation or some value-added activity that produces one or more results.
- It exists because of the result of a prior task (i.e., there is a predecessor/successor relationship to other tasks based on rules or life-cycle expectations).
- It has a responsible person (lead) assigned to that task and has people resources assigned to that work effort.

- A task completion results in earned value for any cost accounting system.
- A task on a schedule is really an instance of a particular task being performed on a different object (i.e., there is a small set of different types of tasks invoked with different objects, such as coding certain things one way and coding other things another way).
- A task "belongs" primarily to a functional thread (i.e., it is primarily an engineering task or a manufacturing task, etc. — even though different roles get involved).
- A task type can be identified statically (i.e., it is an analysis-type task, or a design-type task, or a test-type task, etc.).
- A task type is reusable throughout a project schedule — for both totally different objects and for progressions on the same object (i.e., you can use the same task or activity instance at proposal time and at execution time and leverage work based on that reuse).

In addition, the set of tasks collectively has these characteristics:

- The task instances on a schedule form the entire end-to-end life cycle of work to be done.
- Task instances are really the same process task being performed on different objects within and across project phases.
- Collections of horizontal tasks map to a functional business area (i.e., engineering, manufacturing, management, etc.).

I realized that not all process elements fit nicely into schedulable tasks. The real world must also include all the things that exist to satisfy events that just happen when they happen. These process elements are how-tos that get invoked based on an event or stimulus. Asynchronous events or stimuli do not show up on project schedules. They just occur. The process framework architecture must recognize that these asynchronous events (with their associative how-to process elements) also need to be addressed. You really need to pay attention to accessing these process elements either by event/stimulus, by output/response, or by how-to process element name.

These characteristics fit the process world very well as a basis for connecting process to the real world. There was a problem, however, with some companies (especially older companies) as follows:

- Schedule tasks reflected what the company did over a period of time — regardless of whether the tasks made sense or not.

- Schedule tasks produced things (documents or work products) merely because of the "we've done that for 20 years" mentality. This is the "tribal knowledge" syndrome.
- Schedule task connections were based on convoluted process workflows, developed over years, that were not recognizable from the way they started out.
- Schedule tasks were described as a mix of noun-based items and verb-based items on a schedule (i.e., there was no consistency in representing these activities).

Given these observations, I concluded that although the synchronized real-world connection remained with the project schedule, you needed to look at that schedule to make sure that you were not propagating bad task flows into your process world. There are some interesting indicators that may reflect this phenomenon:

- If the company is personality-driven, this is a good indicator that you may have a process problem. Fred may have done something a long time ago but got moved to another area (and still did everything from before) — even though it is now convoluted. Fred retires and Mary takes over and does what Fred did. After a while, it is set in concrete that that's what Mary does! The process person who questions this is now considered the enemy within.
- Personnel at government contracting companies that have cut their teeth on earlier government standards (like 1679, 2167A, etc.) are so document oriented that this mentality is ingrained into their processes — even though the government has moved on to looser commercial standards! They have lost sight of the fact that engineers produce work products — not documents! Engineers produce things like use case diagrams, sequence diagrams, activity diagrams, UML diagrams, tool-based designs, C++ coding, etc. That's where their training is. They are not English majors and are not good at grammar. They are not document specialists for styles, formatting, boilerplate insertions, and headers or footers. At two companies I worked for, about two-thirds of the engineering workforce were from other countries. English was not even their primary language and yet these engineers found themselves in the (English) document preparation business!
- Within these document-oriented companies described above, another set of detrimental factors emerges that you definitely do not want to continue. The minute you cut and paste a design or other work product result into a document you now have *two* places where that design resides. This is absolutely contrary to any

basic database philosophy of a single location for entities! When the main design gets changed (as it will), you now have to think about where this design also exists. If you're in this mode, you are either guaranteeing extra work to keep things in synch or you have a huge versioning problem where it is unclear which version to trust. The former will add time and costs. The latter can introduce errors and affect quality!

■ Take a look at the existing schedule tasks. If you see a combination of noun-based line items and verb-based line items, be suspicious about the company's real-world process flows. In my process framework architecture, tasks are process activities and represent verb-based actions *period*. The only noun-based schedule items are summary (roll-up) lines that identify things like project spiral identifiers, project increments, project phases, etc. If you see a schedule line item that just has the document name (as a noun), you have double trouble.

■ If you have existing schedule tasks where it is undefined exactly what is being produced, you also have an undefined role in how to get there. What that means is that you have a company that is engaging (or trying to engage) different roles in real time to complete any task. As long as people are around and available, that works. If they are not around or not available, you have a real-world work problem and a real-world process problem.

Given all this, the process person still needs to connect processes to the real world of schedules. The input grist for this effort is existing schedules and availability to interview leads. The process person needs to focus on producing work products and discarding document production. Documents are merely a packaging of work products.

Think about any document. It has a table of contents that identifies what kinds of things exist in each chapter. Typically, the contents of these chapters are dissimilar — the same situation is true for contents in an engineering environment. One section may be Word text, another may be spreadsheet contents, another may be a design representation in graphics, etc. To create a document, you have to package these dissimilar data elements into that document — adding extra effort and costs and replicating data, which can create errors. A far better process approach is to really focus on work products (i.e., each document section) and make no effort to package these data elements into a document. I advocate a separate packaging process activity if you absolutely require a document — that can be charged extra for the extra effort. If you adapt this work product bias to processes, it is absolutely essential that you never get any data from a produced document. You get it from the original work product or tool. I mention this because the amount of time spent producing documents can be enormous. At one company, this effort also caused errors because documents were looked at as gospel when the tool design had moved on. Also, it was pathetic to see engineers who had expertise in programming trying to get documents right with headers and footers, fonts, styles, titles, etc., for which they had no expertise! I saw highly paid people doing really bad jobs that could have been done better and cheaper by others.

To summarize, make document production distinct activities predicated on completion of the parts that make up that document. I am a great believer in the "virtual document" concept where you try to convince your customer to get the real parts directly rather than spending extra effort (and money) in packaging those same parts into a single entity called a document. If your customer insists on a document, the cost of doing this extra (and no value-added) work needs to be factored into your contractual costs. On one project, our financial deliverables were stated as a single document deliverable but we delivered multiple (and separate) files:

- Cover sheets (Word)
- Financial spreadsheet #1 (Excel)
- Financial spreadsheet #2 (Excel)
- Graphic presentation (PowerPoint)

We contacted our customer and said that we planned to send virtual documents at no preparation cost. If he or she wanted real documents, we added time (and costs) in packaging any document for additional pass-on costs. The customer got his or her data at no additional cost and was able to use MS Office applications to directly read these dissimilar data elements. We retained a single data point rather than multiple data sources for higher quality and it cost nothing extra to get the data to the customer.

Having dealt with work products versus documents, here's what you need to do to connect processes to the real world:

- Identify the set of reusable tasks and provide a verb-based action for this process activity. In reality, each activity is identified with a verb-object pair.
- Identify the predecessor/successor types of activities for each named activity. This information comes from both the schedule itself and via lead interviews.

- Map activities to functional threads and project management phases. You want to end up with a clean mapping of activities across the rows (functional areas) and columns (project phases).
- Identify the inputs and outputs for each activity. (This can be gleaned from lead interviews.) Variations need to be ratified. These become part of the stimulus/response story for this process entity.
- Roll up the major stimuli/responses to each Process Activity Diagram (PAD). I talk at length about this later.
- Correlate PAD stimuli/responses to external stimuli/responses. We attack this from middle-up and middle-down perspectives.
- Lastly, identify all the asynchronous events that just "happen" on a get-started how-to process element list.

We have to normalize any existing set of schedules to a set of process activities that are to be reused as different instances operating on different objects on a process-connected schedule. We want to end up with a small "pick list" of process activities whose instances show up on any project schedule. The intent is to have all scheduled tasks be process activities. We want the ability to hyperlink right from a schedule (in addition to other ways of accessing) to a Web-based process activity that tells us our inputs/outputs, our predecessor/successor relationships, our top-level steps, our special training needs, roles involved, any metrics involved, etc. We want to establish a deterministic process entity for each schedule task. How's that for repeatability!

If you haven't realized it up to this point, this process model is based on activities. Another process model is based on work products. This activity-based model can coexist with any work product–based model or tool. The biggest difference between these two fundamental approaches is shown in Table 2.1.

This process model certainly recognizes that you could provide all the lower-level workflows per work product as another process dimension to this model. Whereas this model focuses on the various process elements supporting activities (and their associated elaborated procedures), a work product–based model can provide the low-level workflows per work product. Both can coexist but my thrust is on the activity-based process model.

This is the key to connecting process to the real world.

Table 2.1   Activity Approach versus Work Product Approach

Activity Approach	*Work Product Approach*
Focuses on tasks or activities that relate to work done.	Focuses on work products that relate to work done.
Separates "what you have to do" from "how you are to do it" and allows a mapping of process elements to the model.	Has no such capability. Does support workflows for any particular work product at the work product low level.
Relates one or more work products to any activity.	Has no such connection to schedule task instances.
Allows generic work product terminology at the activity level to support flexibility and extensibility at the work product level.	Work products and their relationships have to be determined up front. There is no such capability of "or" for work products. Extensibility can be constrained.
Does not directly address workflows per work product. Considers this low level and outside the model. This model will support any work product workflow management as an adjunct to this model.	Does address workflows per work product. Can support work product "states" for work product promotion/demotion.
Tight coupling of activities to work products — built in to the model.	Tight coupling of work products to workflow management. Can be set up to tightly couple activities.
Does not require all work products to be totally defined when activities are defined.	Does require all work products to be defined when activities are defined.
Supports the notion that activity execution is more than producing work products (e.g., metrics collection by activity task and task communication for earned value calculation).	Assumes that work product production and activity execution are synonymous.

Chapter 3

The Software Process Model Pyramid

I will address the totality of this pyramid by showing all the dimensions (sides) of this process model beyond the obvious view that practitioners use. I will defer actual implementation aspects (represented by side 4) until Section II. I selected the pyramid to graphically represent the process framework architecture for several reasons. The process architecture has various views or perspectives — represented by the sides of the process pyramid:

- Side 1 is the layered view as seen by day-to-day practitioners/leads/managers.
- Side 2 is the training view that can mirror or encapsulate layers across the entire process repository.
- Side 3 is the process traceability view where we get to connect process elements for compliance purposes.
- Side 4 represents the whole enchilada for the totality of the process repository. It is this last view that gets manifested by the intranet implementation. This gets covered in Section II.

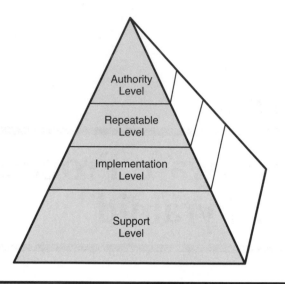

Figure 3.1   Process framework architecture pyramid.

Side 1 of the Software Process Model Pyramid

The view used most by the organization is side 1 of the pyramid subdivided into process layers. These process layers not only separate process types but also separate process customer focus areas. I will discuss this at length later.

The smallest "root node" of side 1 is represented at the top of the pyramid, which I call the "authority" level of the model. This is the very reason why everything else exists. It is this level that is most used by executives to store company policies, maturity models, government regulations, and standards requirements to be followed. In addition to explicit authority requirements, engineering processes have an implied authority that reflects normal engineering life-cycle states. For example, you design something before you code something before you test something. That ordering is just understood in engineering.

The layer right under the authority level of side 1 is the "what you need to do" level or what I call the "repeatable" level. This is bigger than the authority level but smaller than the lower levels. It is this layer that ties the entire process framework architecture to the real world of schedules and project tasking. For this reason, it is appropriately represented high up on the pyramid — but not at the very top. It is this level that is most used by leads/project managers. It is also this level where we want to mandate processes. This is the layer where you achieve process portability. This is the layer where there is a direct connection of scheduled tasks to process activities. This is the layer where static process activity predecessor/successor rules are manifested on a project schedule with activity (task) instances.

The next layer of side 1 is where all the "how we do things" exist. These "how we do things" process entities are called "procedures." Please note that I tend to use two terms interchangeably: "procedures" and "work instructions." In my mind, both are how-tos with work instructions being low-level and detailed whereas procedures can be at any appropriate level of detail. For simplicity, I will use the term "procedures" throughout this book, but a low-level "procedure" can also be a "work instruction." Manufacturing how-tos tend to be called work instructions because they tend to be very detailed. I call this layer the "implementation" level because this is where the "rubber meets the road" for processes. It is this level that is the most used by practitioners. It is also the level where we want extensibility and flexibility at the how-to level. I will show you why the intranet implementation of this layer achieves this in a simple way. In addition to these process artifacts, you place "how selectors" here to support that extensibility and flexibility for procedures. It is this layer that addresses all the supporting procedures from the repeatable level and addresses the event-driven procedural elements.

The last layer of side 1 is what I call the "support" level. This is where all the work product templates, work product inspection checklists, work product guidelines, work product examples, form templates, form inspection checklists, form guidelines, and form examples exist in support of the process elements. You place work product selectors and form selectors here for your Web-based solution. In addition to these process usage records, you also place project-related performance records here to assist in future estimations. Many companies may want to place tools here that support process elements.

Side 2 of the Software Process Model Pyramid

This side is the training view that relates to discrete layers and elements of side 1. Training can exist at the:

- Interprocess layers (e.g., interconnection of one layer to another)
- Process layer level (e.g., end-to-end process repeatability training)
- Individual process element level (e.g., inspection how-to process element training)
- Functional area level (e.g., requirements management that spans layers)

Side 3 of the Software Process Model Pyramid

This side is the process traceability view that covers side 1 layers and side 1 elements along with side 2 training elements. These are the process elements that you show external assessors and auditors. Examples are:

- Company policy compliance matrix
- ISO 9001 compliance matrix
- CMMI compliance matrix
- Government standard compliance matrix
- Government regulation compliance matrix

Some of these compliance matrices also provide an opportunity to map generic compliance roles to your company role equivalents. Similarly, you can map generic compliance work products to your company work product equivalents. A robust compliance mapping of requirements, roles, and objects is an awesome artifact to provide to any external assessor or auditor! You are almost certain to have complete compliance certification! Compliance reaches into various process elements on side 1 of the pyramid and various training packages on side 2. Organizations that are regulated have a potential twist here. If the regulations are true what-level requirements, you have some flexibility in how you satisfy that "what" regulation. If the regulation is a "how," you have no flexibility. In my experience, government entities have a real problem with regulations. They tend to not separate "what you have to do" with selectable how-tos based on some criteria (like the size of a company). With regulated companies, there's a real gotcha in the term "guideline." Some regulating agencies consider this term as a true guide only (i.e., look at the guide but you have the freedom to do something different) whereas others treat this term as an ordained how-to with no variations during implementation.

Side 4 of the Software Process Model Pyramid

This is the side that is represented on the company's intranet. This is the side that has online access to everything represented on the other three sides. This is the Web view of everything. It is here where we place the top-level Web pages that tie all the parts together. It is here that we set up a common accessibility throughout the Web implementation to get to process elements in as many ways as possible. I will talk about this at length in Section II of this book.

Keep this pyramid representation in mind as we proceed farther in understanding this very robust and useful real-world process architecture and methodology.

Chapter 4

The Software Process Model Overview

The Software Process Model Concept

Selectability is a key concept throughout this book because it really addresses tailoring of process entities at all levels of the process framework architecture. Like any architecture design, this also has a "system" design — except we're dealing with process rather than software. Another big aspect of this software process method is that it really is a framework architecture into which process parts fit. The word "fit" is very important, especially because I've seen process elements in place yet people don't know why they're there or they don't know where new process elements fit in the overall scheme of things. Think of a framework as the bones onto which we add the process meat. The beauty of this architectural design is that it separates the framework architecture (in the process specialist domain) from the actual process elements (in the organization's domain). This separation will become a powerful concept later when you organize any process group to populate/control processes in any organization. As Software Engineering Process Group (SEPG) lead and process architect, I concentrated solely on the integrity of the process model whereas the SEPG members concentrated on the actual process elements within that process framework. I have had very successful process groups that have worked effectively and efficiently due to this work separation. I have to admit I led one process group where I was not allowed to make this work separation and it was less than successful — due to a boss who just didn't "get it." This guy was a "my way or the highway" type of individual who had no process background and who insisted on making bad decisions. Any suggestion from me was DOA (dead on arrival) by virtue of it not coming from him. If you are a process person and get into this situation, run fast. You will never succeed. This type of boss will affix blame for all his bad calls on you.

My background (and thus the focus of this book) is software engineering. My examples will draw from that background. I have also applied this process framework model to non–software engineering areas, such as hardware engineering, systems engineering, purchasing, contracts, and human resources areas. The process principles apply just as well to other parts of an organization as they do to the software engineering environment. The principles also apply to totally different organizations such as hospitals, utility companies, and governmental agencies.

Being a software guy in a previous life, I addressed this process architectural framework from a requirements perspective. Here are the basic requirements in lay terms and in no particular order:

- The process approach shall separate what is needed from how things are done.
- The "what is needed" portion of the process approach shall be portable across groups, divisions, sites. (As you see this developed, I maintain that it should even be portable to a subcontractor's process flow on government contracts!)
- The process approach shall directly relate to project or program tasking (i.e., the process world must relate to the real world and vice versa).
- The process "tasks" at the "what" level shall be considered atomic elements with mandated high-level steps to be done (i.e., once a task is selected for execution on a schedule, you do the whole thing — not a part of it!). I say this because one commercial company where I worked routinely ripped key people out of one project to work on another project at the most inopportune times. The resultant disruption was enormous. I also say this because if an activity has eight high-level steps, you do all eight steps — not just the first four or just the last six, etc.
- The process approach shall establish process tasks that are totally selectable for executable instances on a schedule (i.e., schedule task elements are to come from a process "pick list" of "what you have to do" process elements). Your ideal end-position is that any and all tasks on a schedule have process activity counterparts from the process pick list.

- The process approach shall be totally independent of life-cycle methods (i.e., the selection of process "tasks" determines the life-cycle approach). This approach can be used for traditional waterfall life cycles, incremental life cycles, spiral life cycles, or specialized life cycles like the Rational Unified Process (RUP) approach. I do need to point out that each process thread representing differing life cycles may have different process activities pertinent only to that life cycle. Within a life cycle, you should be able to pick and choose process activities where the resultant project schedule reflects a specific variation of that life cycle (spiral versus incremental, for example, within a developmental life cycle).

- The process approach shall be target independent for computer languages, design methodologies, and work products (i.e., you can mix and match C++ programming efforts with C or Ada). You can mix and match object-oriented approaches with functional decomposition. You can get specific with actual work-product binding at either the activity level or the how-to procedural level. I say this because implementation language variations occur at the how-to level. This software process model is great for language selectability at the how-to level in a very natural way.

- The process approach shall recognize that there can be more than one way to do things (i.e., it does not have a one-size-fits-all mentality). This addresses flexibility and tailoring and also supports various tool-set differences at the procedural level. Tools support how-tos. How-tos in this software process model are selectable — therefore, tool support is also selectable.

- The process approach shall inherently encourage better mousetraps (i.e., it will aggressively allow for alternative approaches for extensibility). Don't make it difficult or impossible to consider another way of doing business. Make it easy. With a built-in selectability at the how-to level, it is simple to allow alternative approaches to anything.

- How-to process elements shall be useful. Procedural elements should not be constrained for format or level of detail. Recognize that you don't need how-tos for everything — only those instances where a process element is useful. Please don't wallpaper the process walls with process elements to deal with everything that moves! I must admit that my experience is showing here — people get real upset with useless process elements. You can have low-level equivalents (work instructions) for novices and high-level equivalents (procedures) for knowledgeable users, but don't have process elements exist just for the sake of it.

- The process approach shall have architecture such that process elements have process "homes." Everything has a place in this software process framework architecture. Process names are to be unambiguous as to what they are and where they fit in the process repository. Here's another pet peeve of mine: I've seen horrible piles of process stuff with no rhyme or reason to anything. I may touch a raw nerve here with some people because they will recognize this situation at their workplaces. In these piles of stuff, adding process elements to the pile causes more chaos and makes the elements totally unmaintainable.
- The process approach shall build in traceability of process elements (i.e., there should be no process element that just "floats"). There are actual reasons why process elements exist! With this software process model approach, connectability is built into the model at the working level (pyramid side 1) as well as the training level (pyramid side 2) and compliance level (pyramid side 3).
- Both "what you have to do" process elements and "how you do it" process elements exist based on some inputs (or stimuli) and produce one or more outputs as a response. In this software process method, activities are driven by predecessor activities where data is completed. Procedural elements in this software process method support high-level steps (step stimuli) within any activity or by either inputs or stimuli as asynchronous event-driven process elements.

This chapter is meant to give you a taste of this process framework architecture. Subsequent chapters will elaborate on all the process aspects of this process model. If you don't get it in this chapter, take heart — I will tie all the ends together throughout the book.

This process framework has, at its very core, the separation of "what you do" from "how you do it." The "what you do" process elements are called activities. Activities are schedulable process elements that produce one or more outputs based on one or more inputs. These activities form the entire set of scheduling tasks that appear on all project schedules, which reflect what needs to be done. The "how you do it" process elements are called procedures. I have made a concession in this software process model to the possibility that novice users may need more detail in any how-to than an experienced user. To that end, I have allowed work instructions for that very detailed version of any procedure to recognize these classes of users. Throughout this book, I use the term "procedure" as a common term for a how-to process element. Be aware that some procedures may need a work instruction counterpart. Having said that, be aware that two variations of any how-to creates a potential maintenance problem that needs to be taken into account. Procedures produce one or more outputs as a response to address one of these conditions:

- To elaborate on high-level "what" steps within an activity
- To support a how-to from something in the authority level (policies, standards, maturity models, regulations)
- To support asynchronous business events (or stimuli)

Activities are like scheduling tasks that have predecessor/successor relationships. Each activity produces one or more work products. Because of these traits:

- You can string activities together, showing that predecessor/successor connection relationship.
- You can pick an activity from a process pick list when placing activity task instances on a schedule.
- You have a tight relationship between work products (data) and activities (actions).
- You can have both an activity-based view of the life cycle and a work product–based view of the life cycle. You can even take it to the next dimension by work product and support process flows per work product for role-based involvements and authority signatures.

These connected activities become the entire end-to-end life-cycle story. You can also separate different end-to-end life-cycle stories into major life-cycle approaches by accomodating multiple life cycles. Most software companies need only one life-cycle representation. We'll talk about that later when Web implementation is covered in depth. The point here is that a single company may have a development life cycle versus a maintenance life cycle versus a customer support life cycle, etc. Each life cycle is broken down into phases. One or more phases are life-cycle segments — like the "execution" segment or the "close-down" segment. You might have a development life cycle broken down by developmental and support "swim lanes." Swim lanes are visual aids separating engineering and nonengineering activities. Can you imagine the power of directing users to a swim lane based on their project role? It gets rid of all ambiguity of purpose. Each life-cycle phase has these top-level process entities:

- A process activity diagram, or PAD, that contains the schedulable tasks (activities) within that phase. Each PAD has a specific subset activity life-cycle story for a particular swim lane (e.g., software development life cycle) in a particular life-cycle phase (e.g., implementation phase). These connected activities form the basis for tasks (activity instances) on any project schedule. The totality of the process activities within all PADs becomes the basis for the entire project schedule. I have purposely used "schedulable" (versus "scheduled") because early in life cycles you may not actually schedule an activity in any formal way on a project schedule. Typically, formal project schedules show up after project turn-on — whereas there may or may not be a formal schedule. Note that supporting how-to procedures to activities shown in any PAD are hidden from this layer representation. Only "what you have to do" activities are shown within a PAD.

■ The event-driven list of procedures pertinent to that phase. These are the procedures that have unique how-to solutions based on execution during this particular phase. I realized a long time ago that how-to elements can cover the scope of a single phase and you may need a different how-to for some other phase. This is to address that process eventuality.

■ The event-driven list of procedures that have unique "how" solutions based on the segment that this phase belongs to. Just as above, you need to allow for a segment-based how-to variation. This software process model method accommodates this nicely. For example, a customer requirement change procedure may have a very different "how-to" in a pre-execution segment (proposal time) than during the execution segment (program under contract and live).

■ The event-driven list of procedures that are phase and segment independent. This is the simplest of how-to situations where you have a single how-to regardless of when you execute this procedure throughout any life cycle. An example would be a quality corrective action procedure whose how-to would be the same no matter when it is executed in the life-cycle swim lane.

Let's look at possible process threads that reflect differing major life cycles made up of different segments and phases. Some process life-cycle possibilities might include:

■ Project development life cycle for projects designed, implemented, tested, etc., for the customer — to be used by project management, development management, and engineering

■ Product support life cycle for fielded products — to be used by product support personnel

■ Service life cycle where no products are developed — to be used by service and customer support personnel

- Process development life cycle for process development — to be used by process-group members
- Process support life cycle for process maintenance — to be used by process-group members

I found it desirable to divide a process into subhorizontal subrows (swim lanes) as a visual aid to categorize major organizational functional areas into discrete (and visual) work such as:

- Engineering flow
- Supporting flow

You can accomplish this fundamental separation by color coding process activities but I'm hoping you agree with me that any unambiguous presentation of process is better. For example, you can direct tech writers (support people) to a different swim lane than engineers, who use the engineering swim lane.

Phases in different life cycles may be totally different from other process life cycles or may have the same name. Don't get hung up on this right now. It will become apparent what phases are for any given life-cycle approach. I don't advocate using the same name for segments or phases if the contents of each are significantly different from another same-name entity. That will confuse your process users. I am probably doing a good job of confusing people already without adding software process practitioners to the confusion pool.

I will now show you what a specific PAD might look like. This is depicted in Figure 4.1. The top section of this PAD identifies:

- Which phase we're talking about. It provides a visual indicator showing you where you are in this particular life cycle.
- Horizontal traversal assists to predecessor or successor PADs for the same major life cycle. These are circular buffer pointers where first- and last-phase PADs point to the first and last PADs in the same life cycle. I have not shown vertical traversal in any PAD because that implies traversal to a totally different process life cycle's PAD, which logically does not happen.
- Major inputs to this phase as a one-stop shopping place showing phase-based stimuli. For a process person, these inputs are to show up as activity inputs and vice versa within that PAD. In the Web implementation section, I also advocate tying each phase input to the activity (or activities) that can execute that input as a direct aid to the process user who knows the input but is not aware of where it's processed.

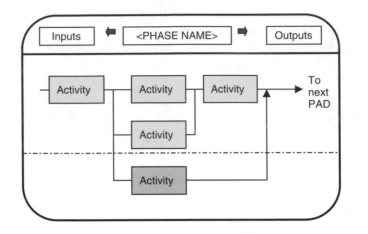

Figure 4.1 Process activity diagram (PAD).

- Major outputs from this phase as a one-stop shopping place, showing phase-based responses. For a process person, these outputs are to show up as activity outputs and vice versa within that PAD. Just as for inputs, I will also advocate tying each phase output to the activity (or activities) that can produce or update that output. This is also a direct aid to the process user who knows an output but is not aware of which activity (or activities) produced or updated it.

The bottom section of the PAD depicts the schedulable process elements and shows two main swim lanes of process information:*

- The engineering process swim lane showing engineering activities
- The supporting process swim lane showing a single support (non-engineering) activity

The end-to-end activities not only tie functional activities together within a PAD but also identify connections to other (horizontal) PADs where other integrated roles are involved at the activity level. It is important to point out that even though an activity inherently "belongs" to a functional thread area, integrated roles can occur *within* that activity at the high-level step to help produce that activity's outputs. These role

---

* I have shown two swim lanes being engineering and support. You may have a different number of swim lanes to reflect your major functional areas of interest.

connections will not show up in the PAD but do show up within the activity's description.

Under each PAD that shows the schedulable process activities, I show the asynchronous or event-driven process elements in the nonschedulable portion. I have called this associative process element the Event-Driven Procedures Lists or EDP lists. There is a one-to-one relationship of any PAD consisting of schedulable tasks to an EDP list consisting of nonschedulable procedures. Let's stop here for a moment to remember what the real world means for process. For any given life-cycle phase, we need to show:

- Schedulable process elements showing predecessor/successor relationships. These show up on project schedules as activity instances or tasks. The PAD represents this.
- Nonschedulable process elements showing the event-driven or asynchronous procedures involved while in this phase time frame. This is the EDP lists area. We show three types of procedural elements in the EDP lists area:
  - Those that have a unique how-to solution if executed during this phase that is different from execution in any other phase.
  - Those that have a unique how-to solution if executed in the life-cycle segment to which this phase is connected. Remember a segment is made up of one or more phases.
  - Those event-driven procedures that are phase independent.

I have shown you what a PAD looks like in Figure 4.1. Lets see what a typical EDP lists area looks like that goes with each PAD. This is depicted in Figure 4.2.

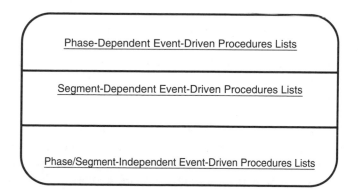

Figure 4.2   Event-driven procedures (EDP) lists.

When we get into the Web implementation section, I will also show where it is desirable to have a variation of this EDP lists area at the top-level life-cycle Web page to aid Web traversal.

These three lists provide multiple ways to find all the asynchronous, event-driven process elements that can occur during that life-cycle phase time frame. The ultimate goal is to quickly locate any event-driven how-to process element.

The very essence of this process approach is shown in the above named figures, namely connecting schedulable processes (activities) to the real world and connecting asynchronous event-based process elements (procedures) to the real world. There are some important points to be made when looking at these depictions:

- Schedules are made up of instances of process activities with the *same* predecessor/successor relationships as shown in all the PADs. This is an important point because the activity flows on a PAD provide excellent insight into mapping instances of these activities (called tasks) on any project schedule. If done right, a project schedule is merely a morphed version of a PAD and vice versa. How about that for connecting the real world to the process world!

- Process activities, once placed on a schedule, bind two more pieces of information to make it a real-world schedule task:
  - The target of the task (activity object)
  - The responsible person (activity lead for this instance)

  Let this sink in. A project schedule line item has three essential elements: the activity name (whose instance is showing up on this schedule); the object (usually the system part) being worked on for this instance; and who's in charge of this project task execution (or activity lead). These three pieces of information uniquely identify the task on a project schedule — even when you have to rework it. In the implementation section, I advocate these three informational elements be three separate columns in your MS Project (or similar) application software to identify the task. By separating these by column, you can hyperlink the activity name directly to the process activity — thus directly connecting project tasking to process activities.

- With any activity connection to a schedule, you can now get to the associated how-to procedures (via how selectors), work product sets (via work product selectors), and form sets (via form selectors) for that process activity. The activity reflects the "what you have to do" process element. The how-to procedural elements that support high-level steps inside the activity are hyperlinked directly from that how selector that in turn is hyperlinked from pertinent high-level steps within any activity. In the implementation section, you'll see that the high-level verbs (that have a how-to elaboration) connect to a how selector that in turn is connected to the how-to selectable process procedures. A similar connectability is seen for work products and forms. The point here is that most things are a click away from references within an activity.

- All the nonschedulable event-driven procedures are also captured in the EDP lists area by phase, by segment, and by life cycle. The combination of these nonschedulable processes (event procedures) and schedulable process elements (activities) forms the totality of processes needed for any given life-cycle phase.
- Finally, all process elements exist because:
  - One or more authority-level process directives or requirements require a process element
  - There is an implied authority-level process directive based on type of business and industry best practices.

The Key Process Element: The Activity

I will talk about the core aspect of this software process model method framework first — the "activity." Activities are schedulable process elements that contain a few high-level steps indicating what needs to be done (not how they are done). Activity instances show up on project schedules as tasks of what needs to be done and are connected to other activity instances showing predecessor/successor relationships shown in the PAD. After giving you a sense of why this is the most important aspect of this software process approach, I will then drill down to the how-to world and the supporting process elements.

First, I have purposely color coded activities in yellow (rather than any other color) to be compatible with a particular project management life-cycle model called PROPS (a general project management model). Yellow was reserved for company processes in that model's "big U." The big U is merely another representation of an entire project management development life cycle. In PROPS, you decompose things down the left side of the U and build things up the other side of the U. Here I merely treated the big U as a bendable coat hanger and straightened it out into a sequence of PADs. It is beyond the scope of this book to describe that particular life-cycle model.

After a complete analysis of schedule tasks, you develop a complete end-to-end story, broken down by phases, where you string together all the activities pictorially showing predecessor/successor relationships among activities. It is this static end-to-end life-cycle story in each PAD that becomes the project schedule, showing the same predecessor/successor relationships between the activity instances to be executed. The activity instances are the schedule tasks of "what needs to be done." You want to end up by closing your eyes, pointing to a schedule task on a schedule, and connecting that task to one of the process activities in the process world.

If you have done your analysis correctly, outputs from one activity should become inputs to another activity. As a process person, I always asked these questions: "Why are you creating some work product?" and "Where does it get used?" In my analysis, I have experienced some work products that were produced with no known consumer. Disconnects like this should provide a red flag that you have a process problem. At one company where I worked early in my career, several listings were routinely produced that had a reason at one point in time but that reason disappeared. At another company, stuff was being sent to someone because his predecessor had needed them in a different role! In both cases, the work products still kept on being produced. You can dig out these kinds of things with this analysis. You will be amazed at how convoluted processes can become over time. I had the dubious honor of producing a "spaghetti chart" for a company's subcontract management processes at one place where I worked. Connectivity between process elements became a big blob over time. I shocked the executives when I showed them this summarized one-pager and defied anyone to follow this mess. The term "spaghetti chart" stuck as part of their culture and was attributed to me.

On a Web implementation, a hyperlink click on any particular activity reference takes you to that activity. I represented that association in the figure by a dotted line in Figure 4.3. This is merely the end-to-end lifecycle way to traverse the Web to get to a particular activity. On my software process method implementations, you can get to this same activity as follows:

- From any activity name list via the common Web "button" on all Web pages
- From the named activity in the phase-based PAD end-to-end lifecycle story (this traversal method)
- From any activity that shows other predecessor/successor activities
- From any activity reference wherever it is

Once at any given activity, you can get to a variety of things as shown in Figure 4.3. At this point, it is merely sufficient to show these associations graphically. In later chapters, each of these process elements will be described fully.

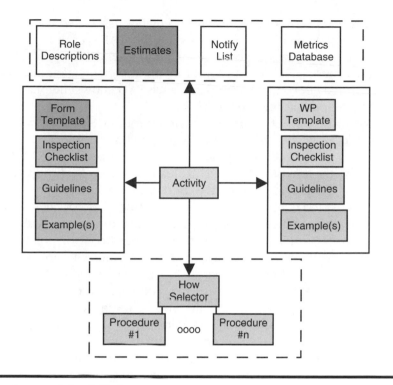

Figure 4.3   Activity drill-down.

There's a top-level world above the process activity. I'll discuss these kinds of things below:

- Any company has one or more major life cycles relevant to their business. In this software process model, each major life cycle is treated as a distinct and separate set of process elements. I have dealt mostly with a development life cycle relevant to software design and development.
- There is an end-to-end process story by major life-cycle phase. This end-to-end story is represented by connected process activities.
- Each major life cycle is divided into segments that in turn are subdivided into one or more phases, which in turn are made up of one or more activities. In the PROPS project management model, an example of a life cycle would be the pre-study segment, the feasibility segment, and the execution segment.
- Each phase contains one or more activities that can be executed in that phase. The depiction of each phase in any life cycle is called a PAD.

- Each PAD shows the connecting activities associated with that PAD along with interfaces to activities in other PADs. Each PAD's activity set is truly a subset to the entire end-to-end life-cycle story and associates activities to a PAD. From an implementation perspective, each PAD becomes a Web page. Each PAD shows the phase inputs and outputs at the PAD level.
- For some project management process models, the between-PAD world is where the major tollgates, major customer reviews, or go/no-go decision points are placed to proceed (or not). Collectively, these types of events are called "major quality gates." The major quality gates themselves become the stimuli to proceed with the next PAD or phase in the life-cycle thread of activities. I worked at one place where the term "gate" almost resulted in fistfights and where we ended up calling these things "control points." I still think that "gate" is an appropriate term because it implies an open or shut condition for these go/no-go situations — but you call them whatever you want. In this software process model, these go/no-go gates occurred at the end of the appropriate PAD.
- Each activity (schedulable task item) is "owned" by a predominant functional area (e.g., an engineering activity) within a PAD and may be reused in different phases (PADs) but still "owned" by the predominant functional area. An example of this process reuse occurs when you need to do a first cut analysis and design to do a proposal in the feasibility segment and then reuse the same activities, building on the proposal effort, in the execution segment!

This is one area of this process framework architecture where I have jumped in to focus on the important role of the activity in this software process model methodology. If you are somewhat lost, I will revisit this topic throughout the book.

To relate the figure to the pyramid model, here's how the following elements relate to the various layers:

- Activities, being "what you have to do," are in the repeatability level of side 1 of the pyramid representation. The end-to-end life-cycle story of activities made up of PADs and individual activity descriptions are all included at that level.
- The how selectors select any procedure and the procedures address "how you do things" — once selected. This software process method feature provides the selectability of how-to procedural elements. These exist at the implementation level of side 1 of the pyramid representation. Remember, because the how-tos are where the "rubber meets the road," we placed them in the implementation

level to reflect that real-world effort. Remember, how-to procedural elements exist to either support high-level steps within any activity or to support asynchronous event-driven events.

■ The work product selectors and form selectors select any work product and form respectively. This software process method feature provides the selectability of work products and forms. Once selected, you get the variation of the work product or form desired. Both the work product sets and form sets exist at the support level of side 1 of the pyramid representation. Each set includes a template, an inspection checklist, guidelines, and example(s). Note: I have shown graphically which ones are mostly optional by using color striping versus solid colors in the figure. Please note that this method associates the inspection checklist with the work product (or form) rather than with the inspection procedure itself! I could never understand why some companies placed these quality checklists with the procedure versus the artifact under inspection. Think about it — if you change the artifact to be inspected, you need to change the inspection checklist. That's why it makes sense to connect these together as part of the set.

■ Things like role descriptions tend to be global in nature and have a scope beyond any one activity. For that reason, these go in the support level of side 1 of the pyramid representation. When we get to the implementation section, you will see that a very simple alphabetically ordered Word file of roles with associated descriptions is what's needed. By placing anchors for each role you can easily hyperlink every role reference to this simple text file. Those process users who need that role description will click on any role name. Those who don't need that information won't bother. The beauty of doing this in a single file is that all roles are in one file for auditing and maintenance purposes.

■ Metrics collections are done by activity. Both collected data and resulting useful information need to be captured. For that reason, these go in the support level of side 1 of the pyramid representation. Please note that any how-to procedure that converts metric data into useful information is like any other how-to procedure and exists at the implementation level. We are talking about the metric data and resulting graphs here that need to be captured for any project and across projects. I talk about this later in the Web implementation section.

■ Estimates, like metrics, need to be collected by project and across projects. I have often thought that the absolute best way of doing this is by directly tying activity instances (tasks) and activity objects to your time-card charging system. This way, you can query your time-card charging system at any time and create resultant useful information in this area. Unlike metrics, you only need the resultant useful information because the data is embedded in your time-card charging system. If you don't tie this software process method of activities to your time-card charging system, you'll need manual data as well. I devote a large part of this book to this area. This is an aspect of the method that is awesome. By doing what I suggest, you can capture how long activities take; create pie graphs showing percentage of time spent in design versus coding versus test, etc.; and you can know the totality of activities spent on any part of your system, etc. You have an incredible database of actuals on which to base future estimations. Companies lose tons of money with bad estimates. This software process model approach addresses this directly.

▪ The notify list is a very special and tailored list based on your company's organization and the level of intelligence you want in this list. This is the part of the software process method that allows you to select who to contact when any activity terminates execution. Some examples are:
  – Next activity lead (responsible person) as shown in the project schedule
  – Project manager
  – Development manager
  – Earned value collection person
  – Quality (for metrics processing)
  – Accounting (for charge number assignments)
  – SCM (for SCM repository expansion)
  This list can be generic (preferred) or can be quite specific (continuous maintenance issue). You have some choices as follows:
  – You can establish a notify list per activity
  – You can establish a global notify list

If you have a list per activity, it makes sense to associate this list at the repeatability level of side 1 of the pyramid representation to go with the activity definition. If you have a global list, it makes sense to associate this list at the support level of side 1 of the pyramid representation. You get to this list via the high-level "end" step in all activities. To be consistent with the software process model, "end" takes you to a how selector that in turn takes you to a how-to procedure that has your contact list.

Chapter 5

Side 1 — Level 1 Authority Level

Authority Level

The basic questions to be answered are "why is this process element there?" and "what does it fulfill?" in your organization.

The point here is that process elements should have a reason for being. These reasons usually include:

- Fulfilling that industry's developmental life cycle
- Fulfilling company policies
- Complying with international standards like ISO 9001
- Meeting maturity models like the CMMI
- Complying with government regulations
- Complying with industry regulations

There should be no process elements that are just there and serve no purpose other than that someone felt the urge to write them. There is a huge caveat when dealing with implied authority requirements. These implied directives are based on the type of business you're in. All process elements should be there to directly support one (or more) authority-level element.

The authority level is where you place all the reasons why:

■ Activities exist in the repeatable level (side 1)
■ Procedures exist in the implementation level (side 1)
■ Work products/forms exist in the support level (side 1)
■ Training packages exist (side 2)

You connect the dots for total connectivity from the authority level to any process element in the compliance portion of this software process model methodology (side 3).

Given that explanation, you place all the top-level "what" requirements or process bases in this level. These are the types of things that go in this authority level:

■ Company policies
■ ISO 9001
■ Government/industry regulations
■ CMM or CMMI
■ Six Sigma (DMAIC/DMADV)

Of this list, all of them are external documents except company policies. Try to get electronic copies of all external documents so that you can extrapolate compliance matrices for them.

A company policy should be a short high-level assertive statement that, from a process perspective, is a high-level "what" requirement. In one implementation, I had suggested that an ISO 9001–certified company consider the ISO standard requirements as the foundational basis whereas company policies supplemented those ISO 9001 requirements. *It is a mistake to have any company policy replicated in any ISO 9001 requirement.* If this supplement approach were followed, the company policies would be small in number and be organized in the same areas as ISO 9001. At one company, I felt their policies, which numbered in the hundreds, could be condensed down to two pages given this philosophy of allowing ISO 9001 to be the foundation. For ISO 9001–compliant companies, your company policies should:

■ Elaborate on an existing ISO 9001 requirement for a company-specific directive
■ Supplement ISO 9001 requirements for company-specific topics

One place where I worked mixed up their company policies with procedures and titles. Some policies weren't even high-level assertive statements! They mixed "whats" and "hows" and committed the cardinal sin of placing titles in a process artifact. This same company routinely reorganized every few years so the embedded titles were almost always wrong or nonexistent. When you write a company policy statement, keep in mind that it is a 40,000-foot level requirement with no how-to connotation. The end result should conjure up "what part of this don't you understand?" in your mind. Write each policy statement as a "shall" statement.

In all instances, we will end up with a collection of authority-based process elements that we must "answer the mail" about. Side 3 of this process model is where we make that connection between the authority level and the process elements that meet those requirements. These connections in side 3 take the form of compliance matrices to show senior management, auditors, and assessors that we have complete traceability throughout the process repository. In one company, I actually had to argue the case that compliance matrices made sense and should be provided to external ISO 9001 auditors and others. They wanted to keep this under wraps. Hard to believe, eh? If you really want to be certified, this will do it in spades!

This level is important to tie all the ends together throughout the process world but typically is unused by the process practitioners and leads. They will use the other levels of side 1. This authority level associated with side 3 (all the compliance matrices) is primarily maintained by the process group and used for certification, external auditors, external CMMI assessors, and government regulators.

I would be remiss if I did not mention that the reasons why processes exist fall into two general categories:

- To support the very essence of your day-to-day business
- To be compliant with imposed or necessary standards/maturity models that support new business acquisition (and make your company run better)

The former is an implied authority; the latter is an explicitly stated authority. There is no specific authority beyond company policies. You will see only company policies in this authority level.

As your business develops, the way you do things as a garage shop operation is radically different from when your staff grows and grows. I know of one company chairman of a fairly large company who still has the same mindset as when the company was small. You constantly run into "why can't you just get five people in a room, bang heads to solve any problem, and get it all fixed tomorrow?" kind of thinking. Can you imagine trying to be a successful process person in that environment?

Chapter 6

Side 1 — Level 2 Repeatable Level

End-to-End Life-Cycle Diagram (Repeatable Level — Side 1)

Any end-to-end life-cycle diagram is really a set of conjoined phases represented as horizontal process activity diagrams (PADs). On the upward side, one or more contiguous phases can also be grouped together as life-cycle segments that in turn become the entire life cycle. On the downward side, each PAD contains a partial life cycle represented by process activities showing predecessor/successor relationships among activities.

More than one life-cycle representation is merely another row of consecutive PADs. If you're really smart about this, any and all alternative life cycles can be mapped onto a common set of segments. If not common, each alternative life cycle has a different segment mapping. Any entire end-to-end life-cycle story would be overwhelming on a single, large, long sheet of paper. Multiple life cycles would be even worse. In the software process method, we subdivide any entire end-to-end story into manageable chunks (called PADs), which can also be individual Web pages for visibility. An example of a single PAD can be seen in Figure 4.1. Figure 6.1 is merely another view of this from a large piece of paper perspective.

Figure 6.1   End-to-end life-cycle diagram.

Any end-to-end life-cycle diagram can be thought of conceptually as a large piece of butcher paper showing all the activities with their predecessor/successor relationships for all functional areas from cradle to grave. You address all the concurrent engineering aspects of integrated roles when mapping out these end-to-end tasks. Each PAD is organized such that certain major functions like engineering versus support (see Figure 4.1) can further be shown as threads of activities that go across the paper (rows). This software process model method calls these sub-rows process "swim lanes" to provide a visual aid to these major engineering and support functions. Each PAD has these additional pieces of information:

- Inputs (i.e., stimuli to the phase or PAD)
- Outputs (i.e., responses from this phase or PAD)
- PAD-to-PAD traversal aids

In addition to a PAD per phase to encapsulate all the schedulable tasking activities, each phase also has an EDP (event-driven procedures) lists area. These contain the asynchronous events that are not schedulable tasks but processes that can be executed based on some stimuli and that produce some responses.

The combination of the PAD and EDP per phase contains all the processes that you need and serves as the high-level or phase-based Web page for our process engine. It also serves as a one-stop shopping location for your major inputs and outputs, schedulable tasks, and asynchronous events — thus treating the entire life-cycle diagram as a black box.

If you now step back and look at segments across a life cycle, these are the major columns of your high-level Web page. To remind you about segments, these are things like "pre-planning," "feasibility," "execution," and "maintenance" in one model or "pre-proposal," "proposal," "execution," and "close-out" in another model. Each segment can be made up of one or more phases and are thus merely segment columns subdivided further into subcolumns. If you look at individual life cycles, these are the major rows of your high-level Web page. Functional areas within a life cycle are merely major rows subdivided into subrows.

Depending on the project management model for a single life-cycle representation, you may end up with four to six major segments (or columns) for each company or enterprise. The major row heading would be the name of the specific life cycle broken into two schedulable swim lanes, for example:

- Engineering
- Support

Notice the use of the word "schedulable." Engineering and support can both have schedulable tasks across life-cycle segments and phases. They can also have nonschedulable process procedural elements that we can show in the appropriate EDP. The CMMI also talks about project management. Typically, project management–related processes are not schedulable but show up wholly in the EDP areas. For that reason, I have excluded project management as a schedulable swim lane.

I do want to point out that some companies might like to break "engineering" into "system engineering," "software engineering," and "hardware engineering." Also "support" can be "quality," "documentation," and "configuration management." My take on this is that this further breakdown merely complicates your Web presentation with little to no value. I recommend you don't make that further breakdown. I found that two major swim lanes were sufficient for the most part. As you increase these functional area subrows, you get more and more sparseness in each PAD. All the functional areas have asynchronous aspects to them beyond any schedulable tasking. We can handle all those types of things under the EDP lists for each phase, segment, or life cycle. General management processes tend to be exclusively asynchronous by nature rather than schedulable by nature. These get handled under the EDP for the appropriate phase, segment, or life cycle.

The major top-level column headings should mirror the project management life-cycle model that your company is following. For one company where I worked, the PROPS project management model was followed — so the column headings were:

- Pre-study segment
- Feasibility segment
- Execution segment
- Conclusion segment

Each segment above is made up of one or more phases. In a Department of Defense (DoD) contracting environment, the life-cycle model may be something like:

- Pre-proposal segment
- Proposal segment
- Start-up segment
- Execution segment
- Close (or wrap up) segment

If you do this correctly, the following items are true:

- Life-cycle phased tollgates, major reviews, or major go/no-go decision points occur at the end of any PAD or phase and prior to the following PAD or phase (i.e., these are essentially between-PAD decision points in this software process model method). For consistency, I advocate that we show these decision points at the end of a PAD rather than at the front of the next one. In the programming world, this is analogous to the "Do <PAD activities> while" statement.
- Any PAD is composed of a set of 1…n connected activities (i.e., the process activity is the atomic element where any activity output is an input to another activity). Ideally, each activity within a PAD is noninterruptible when executed on a project schedule. At one company, they routinely ripped out key people from one project to bolster another project right in the middle of a scheduled activity and then wondered why they had huge problems with process integrity.
- Interfunctional area inputs and outputs have connections from activities in one functional area (swim lane subrow) to the same or another functional area (swim lane subrow) within any PAD. This is a visual way to connect support activities with nonsupport activities where it is absolutely clear what drives what.
- The project schedule, made up of activity instances, should track to the appropriate end-to-end life cycle showing predecessor/successor relationships across a series of PADs. The project schedule should further track process swim lanes as depicted in each PAD to clearly show main activity tasking from supporting activities. If done correctly, each PAD depiction provides an incredible road map to develop any project schedule.

From a mapping perspective:

- A PAD is made up of 1…n schedulable activities connected as predecessor/successor activities.
- Horizontal PADs represent an end-to-end story for any given life-cycle model.
- Major go/no-go decision points or major reviews effectively occur between PADs but are shown at the back end of any PAD.

- All asynchronous process aspects by phase, segment, or life cycle show up in the appropriate EDP list connected to each PAD.
- Global asynchronous process aspects show up at the high level where all PAD references exist.
- Each and every activity can belong to an activity group to get metrics on how efforts are being spent, regardless of where the activity shows up on the end-to-end process depiction. Examples may be activities called "design down" (for system and subsystem designs) and "design unit" (for end-unit design) that are all part of the design activity group for metrics purposes. If it's not obvious by now, these activity groups are statically determined by type of activity. Another type of metric is gathered when you apply the activity object at execution time to determine total effort for a specific piece of the system.
- Project schedule tasks should map directly to process activities in each PAD. There should be no schedule task that is not a process activity. Predecessor/successor relationships on a project schedule should exactly match those relationships shown on any PAD.
- All activities can map directly to your time-charging system. This is where you really get tremendous power with this software process model method. Consider a time-card charging number that is composed of these subelements:
  - <Project ID> part — one unique number for each active project
  - <Process Activity ID> part — one unique number for each process activity
  - <Process Activity Object ID> part — one unique part number per system
  - <Rework ID> part — defaulted at "0" for initial work, 1...9 for reworked efforts in a circular fashion

With this charge number you can get incredible metrics gathered directly from your time-card system that can provide pie graphs and actuals for any piece of your total system. When estimating effort for future contracts, you now have a real basis from which to develop new estimates. Also, you get more and more robust at little to no cost — because your time-card system can always reestablish valuable metric information.

Ideally, you want your time-card charging system aligned with activities in this model. Because instances of activities are schedule tasks, you can get a lot of mileage out of this time-card alignment.

Without that accounting support, you can do a poor man's version of this by setting up a catchall document per activity for actuals to be saved. This would require the responsible person to add something to that document after any activity is done to capture certain actuals that might be useful for future estimations:

- Number of people doing the task (i.e., team size)
- Experience levels involved
- Elapsed time to do the activity
- Actual time elements to do in total (hours/weeks)
- What object you were working on

This metrics capture does not need to be a work of art, just useful.

Process Activity Diagrams (PADs) (Repeatable Level — Side 1)

There is exactly one PAD for each phase in each life cycle. As a reminder, a PAD shows the schedulable tasks in any project schedule.

The concept behind the PAD is that people get overwhelmed with too much information all at once — if you only had the entire end-to-end diagram. If you're an engineering lead or in a management role, you mainly need to look at the engineering swim lane of any PAD. If you're a project manager, you need to look at all swim lanes in all PADs. If you're in a particular phase, you only need to look at that phase's activities.

The human pitfall of the PAD swim-lane concept in this method is that people tend to think "organization," rather than functional area. Your company organizational structure may or may not line up with a particular swim lane within a PAD. You may have multiple organizations share a swim lane. For example, system engineering, hardware engineering, and software engineering may all share the engineering swim lane. This software process model is very much against any stove piping related to organizations and emphasizes integrated role involvement by functional area topic. The reason for this is simple: Organizations come and go whereas functions exist as constants. The beauty of the PAD concept from a presentation perspective is that one PAD equals one Web page.

Each PAD has these pieces of information:

- External inputs to this whole PAD
- External outputs from this whole PAD
- Left/right traversal to other PADs in the life cycle — as a circular horizontal buffer
- A mini–life cycle showing a partial end-to-end story related to that life-cycle phase divided into functional swim lanes
- Connections to other PADs where hand-offs occur to other PADs

Event-Driven Procedures (EDP) Lists (Repeatable Level — Side 1)

There is a one-to-one mapping of an EDP lists area per PAD. The lists themselves are part of the repeatable level because things show up during places in the life cycle. The referenced procedures are at the implementation level. These lists show all the asynchronous process how-tos or procedures by phase, segment, or life cycle. A major part of this software process method is to recognize that not all process elements are schedulable! You may have to follow a process at one phase or segment that is different in another phase or segment. The software process method provides total flexibility and selectability to address all the permutations and combinations necessary for process compliance.

For each phase, you'll see an EDP lists area composed of:

- Phase-based procedures list. These are procedures that apply only to this phase.
- Segment-based procedures list. These are procedures that apply only to this segment.
- Life cycle–based procedures list. These are procedures that are phase/segment independent and apply to the entire life cycle.

This is the part of the software process method where I advocate replication of event-driven procedural references. A procedure that is to apply to a given segment will show up in all phases for that segment as a replicated procedure reference. A procedure that is to apply to the entire life cycle will show up in all phases or segments as a replicated procedure reference. You want to set these lists up so that it is absolutely clear which flavor of procedure is involved at this part of the life cycle. Never introduce ambiguity by presenting two (or more) flavors of a procedure to the process user.

End-to-End Life Cycle of Activities

The primary focus in developing this end-to-end approach centers on the activities. The entire set of activities, once strung together showing predecessor/successor relationships and portioned into PADs, becomes the "end-to-end life cycle." Activities are predetermined process "what you have to do" tasks whose instances are placed on a schedule and become schedule tasks. Schedule tasks, like process activities, have predecessor/successor relationships to each other. I will show an example of the kind of end-to-end life-cycle process story that I'm talking about and its

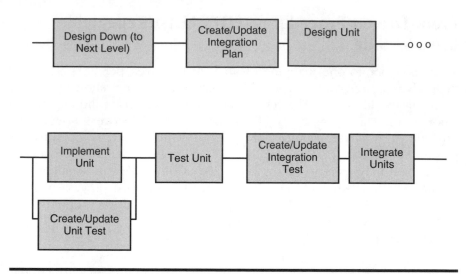

Figure 6.2   Partial process activity diagram (PAD).

associated schedule. I will show just the end-to-end life-cycle portion (snippet) related to the example in Figure 6.2. The full end-to-end life cycle is the one that you need to show on the intranet.

Figure 6.2 is a partial representation of a PAD that you would see on the process Web site. I have purposely omitted nonactivity information you would see in any PAD and concentrated just on the activities themselves. There are some general points to be made about these activities:

- The diagram shows which activities can exist before and after other activities. For example, "create/update integration test" has to be done prior to "integrate units." Also, "test unit" can have the predecessor activities "implement unit" and "create/update unit test" both done as precursor activities. These same two activities can be done in parallel.
- What is not explicitly shown but implied in this software process model approach is that any process activity can be bypassed totally — when it makes sense to do so. Remember that an activity is an indivisible atomic element. Once selected for a schedule, you execute the whole thing, not a part of it. For example, if you have truly reused units (produced and tested before), you can bypass "implement unit," "create/update unit test," and "test unit" activities. You would still want to integrate any reused unit, however. In the real world, some reusable code does in fact need tweaking. In that instance, all these activities would exist to handle the "tweaked" portion of the coding. This process framework

architecture makes no effort to show all the combinations and permutations of activity bypasses that address all the variations to the theme. I leave that up to the project manager or development manager as a commonsense issue.

This static representation shows several things to aid predecessor/successor placement of activities when placed on a schedule for execution as follows:

■ "Design Down (to next level)" is done before "Create/Update integration plan." I purposely did not call this activity "Design Down (to some name)" because a decomposing type of design activity is the same process element whether you go from systems to subsystems or subsystems down to units, etc. By implying "next level," I do not need nomenclature for all the decomposed parts of the system. Also, whenever you get better visibility on any level of design, you need to revisit the integration plan and revisit the program schedule. Think about it — you can't integrate parts of the system until you know what they are. You don't know that until after you do a design activity. In other words, the output of the "design down" type activity is an input to any integration plan. There's another extremely important aspect of any design type of activity that is not evident. Once you execute a "design down" type of activity that gives additional visibility to the lower-level decomposed parts, you can use this output to dictate the activity instances on a schedule! If you execute a "Design Down" activity at the system level, the resultant design will tell you how many subsystems you have exactly. You now know for sure how many more "Design Down" activities you'll need on your schedule (i.e., one per designed subsystem). If you execute a "Design Down" activity on subsystem ABC and determine there are three (not two or four) decomposed units (or components), you know for sure that you'll need three schedule threads of activities related to those units as a result of the design. Think about what I just said about a design type of activity that provides additional visibility on the parts. You get a 3-for-1 deal out of it: *The design is used as input to lower-level design or implementation, real insight into what the enfolding schedule looks like, and expands your charge number assignment.* You want the actual project schedule tasks to be true to the real world. This process method provides that process connection to ensure that reality. Your original plan (based on estimations) may have (and usually does have) a different part story than what your real designs are calling for on this process-based schedule. To the project managers out there, don't get wrapped around the axle about this discrepancy between plan (estimated schedule) and actual (real schedule). I actually experienced a project manager going berserk when the estimated part story was different than what the design actually called out! This software process method advocates delaying schedule tasks (process activity instances) until you know the results of your decomposed design and your integration plans. We want the instance count of any process activity to be based on reality.

■ "Create/update integration plan" is probably the most important activity — next to the design activities mentioned above. You'll notice that I used both "Create" and "Update" as the action verb choices. That was done on purpose. This activity can be executed to create an integration plan and it can be executed to update an existing integration plan. With this activity you should consciously plan out how you're going to integrate all the parts of the system ahead of time. *This integration plan work product drives the implementation order of units and integration testing of those units.* The software process method allows scheduling to be very intelligent and allows for just-in-time tasking based on developed plans. Existing designs can also be fed into the creation/updating of any integration plan. It is desirable to execute this activity after each execution of any "Design Down" type of activity — especially the last instance that identifies the unit "leaves". The reason for this is simple: You have better visibility of the parts story after you execute any "Design Down" activity. Execution of any "Design Down" activity provides better visibility on low- and lower-level parts. If you don't execute, you have an integration plan that does not keep up with your design and is wrong or incomplete at any given point in time. Keep your integration plan as close to the real time of your design as possible. From a "process guy" perspective, failing to do this can cause process errors.

■ The "Design Unit" activity is the low-level design that does not result in any lower-level design. It is the end-design type of activity. I took the liberty of using the term "unit" to reflect the lowest level of design that needs coding. You may use another term if that does not agree with your company terminology for end units. Your top-level designs (from "Design Down" activities) should specify both the unit count and which ones are reused versus which ones are to be built. I mention this because the "Design Down" type activity also specifies clearly which units require a "Design Unit" (to-be-built units) and which ones don't (reused units). This process method's "Design Down" work products provide not only that end-target system design but also provide intelligence related to scheduling "Design Unit" activities (or not) based on that design.

■ The "Implement Unit" activity is where you actually code these low-level components. Because each activity has a built-in inspection step, the completed code is inspected before you can finish it. This model always inspects the completed work products, whether documents or code or whatever, as part of completion. For code, this means that you have inspected code as a minimum before entering unit test or integration test. I mention this because unit testing may not be done for embedded coding or for fast-paced commercial coding environments. The successor activity is the "Test Unit" activity. The "Create/Update Unit Test" activity is shown as being a possible concurrent activity. For schedule executions, you will need one "Implement Unit" for each unit that is to be code touched, whether full implementation or partial implementation on legacy/reused code units. You get the number of possible units from your "Design Down" activities. You also get which are reused totally or partially or are new coding from these same designs. Designs drive the look and feel of the schedule.

■ The "Create/Update Unit Test" activity is where you develop the unit test driver/harness to do any unit test. The term "unit" may be "classes" for C++, or "Ada Packages" for Ada development, or "components," etc. You only need these types of activities on those units that will undergo unit testing. Notice that the "Test Unit" successor activity requires both code to be there and the test driver to be there before you can do any unit test. If you don't do a unit test for any unit, you don't need this activity as well. If you are panicking now, remember that this software process method has a built-in inspection step in all activities as part of declaring it "done." Any implemented unit will have undergone a code inspection whether tested or not. I can personally attest to certain classes of software that definitely do not lend themselves to unit testing (with all the accompanying costs and efforts) but do require code inspections.

■ The "Test Unit" activity is where you actually run the (inspected) unit test driver against the (inspected) unit code. This kind of low-level test can be instrumented as white-box or black-box testing to make sure the unit of coding is behaving as it should. Unit testing is expensive and should be restricted to mission-critical units, customer-focused units of concern, and possibly reused units for confirmation purposes. With this method you can forego unit testing and still achieve high quality by virtue of inspections built into all activities.

■ The "Create/Update Integration Test" activity is where you actually develop the integration tests as determined by the integration plan. You will have deduced by now that if you have a unified target design work product, and integration planning is tied to design, you can also include that integration plan with your design as an integrated work product (i.e., the integration plan and your system/subsystem design can be one and the same as a work product). Also notice that this activity is connected to the "Integrate Units" activity. You can't actually test any sets of units until you have the integration test approaches done. You will have both of these on a schedule for as many integration sets of units as described in the integration plan. For example, if the integration plan lays out that we will integrate units A, B, and C first, then integrate that base with units D and E, and finally integrate that base with unit F — then you will have three instances of this activity on a schedule. The first instance shows up after units A, B, and C are ready to be integrated; the second after units D and E are ready to be integrated *and* the base is ready; and the third after unit F is ready to be integrated along with the expanded base. This is yet another reason why the integration plan is really important. You can intelligently implement and test the earlier needed units early and defer implementation and test of later needed units to later — all based on information gleaned in the integration plan. By being smarter about this, you can actually shorten the time to market and reduce the life cycle's elapsed time by intelligently allowing this activity-based software process model to manage your execution schedules.

■ The "Integrate Units" activity is where you perform integration testing on the integration sets specified by the integration plan. The exact number of these instances on a project schedule is described in the integration plan. This software process method has a very interesting notion about plans — you actually follow them by having the project schedule reflect any plan. Unlike the 2167A world I was in for a hunk of my life, plans were considered as mere deliverables to the government and were not necessarily followed.

To really cement this in, let's play "small project" right now. Here's the scenario:

My design calls out that I have six units identified as units A, B, C, D, E, and F.
My software plan calls out that Unit B does not have to be implemented or tested because I have legacy coding that can be

used as is. Unit C also exists but needs tweaking and unit testing. Units A, D, E, and F all need to be totally implemented but only unit A is considered critical for unit testing whereas units D, E, and F will just be integrated as inspected code.

My integration plan calls out that I will integrate these units as follows:

Integrate A, B, and C as one integration set.

Once that is done, integrate units D and E as the second integration set.

Once that is done, integrate the last unit F into that base. This third integration set is made up of a single unit to be integrated.

Notice that I have used my project plans and designs to actually drive the schedule! What a concept to actually use these work products beyond something to satisfy management or contract demands!

You need to execute certain activities before you really know what successor activities exist. This is contrary to most project management thinking where you lay out all activities at once, whether it's true or not. I separate out "planning packages" from "work packages" on schedules. Planning packages are merely estimates on what the schedule may look like — usually shown as large summary blocks to reflect planned effort. Work packages in this model are instances of activities on a schedule and are only placed there when you know for sure that they are to exist. *This means that you simply cannot place all work package activities on a schedule until plans and designs say so.* Project managers have a real problem here in separating planned versus actual depictions of schedules, because the schedules may look different. A project manager once came unglued when the actual number of units turned out to be different than what was estimated. This project manager was so irate that the developers forced their design into the "right" number even though it was a bad decision and created havoc later in good design, test, performance, and documentation.

Let's see what our schedule would look like at different times in this life cycle — just by using the activities described above. We'll look at the schedule progression at these points in time:

- Up to and including creating the integration plan (see Figure 6.3). We will know the units from the design and will know how to integrate those units. We also know that we have to create that integration plan after design anyhow.
- The balance of the schedule. This schedule story unfolds as a direct result of our design and plan.

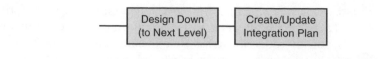

Figure 6.3   Up to and including the integration plan.

After executing the "Design Down (to next level)" activity, we now understand that we have six units named A, B, C, D, E, and F. Planning package estimations may have predicted five or seven — but our design knows for sure now that it's six. We can use that intelligence to expand our actual (work packages) schedule. We know we'll have six unit-related threads on the schedule. We should know which require unit designs, which require unit tests, which are legacy/reused units, which need tweaking, etc.

After executing "Create/Update Integration Plan," we now complete that schedule story for each unit. We also know how many integration sets we have and the order of integration. Can you imagine the power this gives you?

- Order implementation of units to match the plan (i.e., place units early that are to be implemented early in the schedule). Delay implementation of units to be integrated to later in the schedule. You can actually accomplish "just-in-time" scheduling to really shorten your schedule with this software process model!
- Know exactly when integration happens for maximization and concurrency of integration efforts.

Let's now turn our attention to the schedule thread for unit A. I will repeat here what we know about unit A:

- It is to be totally designed and implemented.
- It needs to be unit tested because it's a critical unit.
- It is part of the first integration set.

Based on that information, our schedule thread for unit A now looks like Figure 6.4.

Please note the following about this portion of the schedule related to unit A:

- I've added "(A)" to the schedule instances to bind the activity to the object (in this case, "unit A") for this graphical depiction. In reality, I have had three schedule columns in tools like MS Project for each schedule task (process activity instance) that show:

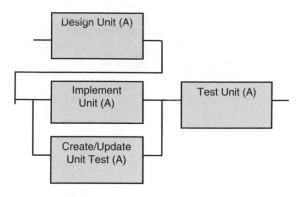

Figure 6.4   Unit A schedule thread.

- Activity name (e.g., "Implement Unit"). This is where I can hyperlink the activity name directly to the process activity on the intranet. This is an incredible coupling of schedule tasking to the process activity for that real-world connection.
- Activity object name (e.g., "A"). This is a variant at process activity execution time that uniquely ties the activity to what it's working on — primarily the part of the system. This separate piece of information accommodates interesting metrics on various efforts applied to those parts of the system.
- Activity responsible person (e.g., "Mary Green"). Like the object above, this identifies the lead for this schedule task to aid uniqueness and to provide interesting metrics by person. This field also provides a real person's name for activity initiation notification.

■ This representation shows that the actual unit test driver development *can* happen concurrently with unit development if you have the resources to do this. If you don't have the people resources, these may need to be executed serially with the unit test driver developed after unit implementation. Remember the process depiction is ideal by definition. Real-world resources (or a lack of resources) may cause parallel activities to be done one after the other instead, in reality.

■ This representation clearly tells you that to actually test the unit, you need both the unit code under test and the unit driver (i.e., the "Test Unit (A)" schedule task [or activity instance] has two predecessor tasks). Because inspections happen in all activities, you have a high degree of quality of both the unit test harness and the coding under test — before you even do any testing.

■ This whole thread completion for unit A is one of three predecessor thread efforts that need to occur before you can do any integration type of activity. The later integration requires units A, B, and C all to be complete before execution.

Let's now look at the schedule thread for unit B. I will repeat here what we know about unit B:

■ It is legacy coding.
■ It can be used as is with no unit design, coding, or testing.
■ It is part of the first integration set.

Based on that information, our schedule thread for unit B now looks like Figure 6.5 (i.e, null).

Figure 6.5   Unit B schedule thread.

Please note the following about this portion of the schedule related to unit B:

■ This (null) representation merely notes that unit B is part of the first integration set but has no unit level efforts involved. Real-world projects may not show a null line but may reflect the end result that unit B is good-to-go for integration. Having said that, I can make the case that a null representation explicitly shows that unit B is considered, rather than wondering about it.

Let's now turn our attention to the schedule thread for unit C. I will repeat here what we know about unit C:

■ It is legacy coding.
■ It needs additional code tweaking that does not affect design.
■ It needs to be unit tested.
■ It is part of the first integration set.

Based on that information, our schedule thread for unit C now looks like Figure 6.6.

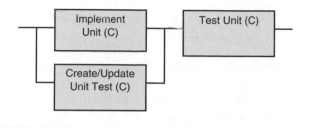

Figure 6.6   Unit C schedule thread.

Please note the following about this portion of the schedule related to unit C:

- I've added "(C)" to the schedule instances to bind the activity to the object (in this case, "unit C") for this graphical depiction.
- This representation shows that the actual unit test driver development *can* happen concurrently with unit development if you have the resources to do this. If you don't have the resources, these will need to be serially developed with the unit test driver after unit implementation.
- This representation clearly tells you that to actually test the unit, you need both the unit code under test and the unit driver (i.e., the "test unit C" schedule task [or activity instance] has two predecessor tasks).
- This whole thread completion for unit C is one of three predecessor thread efforts that need to occur before you can do any integration type of activity. The later integration requires units A, B, and C all to be complete before execution.

Depending on whether units A or C get implemented and tested first or second, you will now be able to place the first integration-type activity on the schedule as shown in Figure 6.7.

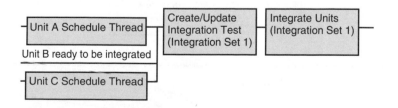

Figure 6.7   Integration set 1 schedule thread.

There are several points to be made about this segment of the schedule:

■ To provide a big-picture view, I purposely used single boxes to represent units A and C threads rather than clutter up this figure.

■ You can't do the "Create/Update Integration Test" activity until all elements of the first integration set are "done." The integration plan specified all this.

■ Notice the object specified in the integration-type activities is "Integration Set 1." This should exactly match what was specified in the integration plan. Also, the schedule reader will get a visual insight into the integration plan by clearly showing that units A, B, and C are indeed integration set 1.

I haven't talked about units D, E, and F yet. Because our integration plan clearly spelled out that units A, B, and C are to be in integration set 1, we know that we can tackle those units early in the schedule. We also know that units D and E are to be in integration set 2 and therefore we can defer those unit threads on a schedule until after units A, B, and C are done. Unit F is not needed until even later, so it can be deferred. Let's now take a look at units D and E that make up integration set 2.

I will repeat here what we know about unit D:

■ It is to be totally designed and implemented.
■ It does not need to be unit tested.
■ It is part of the second integration set.

Based on that information, our schedule thread for unit D now looks like Figure 6.8.

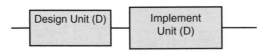

Figure 6.8   Unit D schedule thread.

Please note the following about this portion of the schedule related to unit D:

- I've added "(D)" to the schedule instance to bind the activity to the object (in this case, "unit D") for this graphical depiction.
- There is no unit test or test driver activity needed — just the implementation. You are reminded that this process architecture has a built-in inspection in each and every activity. This means that even though there is no unit test, you do have the implemented code inspected.
- This whole thread completion for unit D is one of two predecessor thread efforts that need to occur before you can do any integration type of activity for integration set 2. Integration set 2 requires units D and E both to be complete before execution.

Let's now turn our attention to the schedule thread for unit E. Unit E is very similar to unit D. Based on that information, our schedule thread for unit E now looks like Figure 6.9.

Please note the following about this portion of the schedule related to unit E:

- I've added "(E)" to the schedule instance to bind the activity to the object (in this case, "unit E") for this graphical depiction.
- There is no unit test or test driver activity needed — just the implementation. The code has been inspected, however.
- This whole thread completion for unit E is one of two predecessor thread efforts that need to occur before you can do any integration type of activity for integration set 2. Integration set 2 requires units D and E both to be complete before execution.

Depending on whether units D or E get implemented first or second, you will now be able to place the second integration-type activity on the schedule as shown in Figure 6.10.

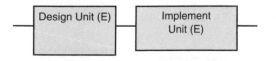

Figure 6.9   Unit E schedule thread.

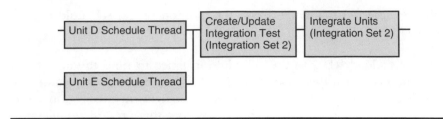

Figure 6.10   Integration set 2 schedule thread.

It is important to note that you can't integrate set 2 until integration set 1 has been integrated and tested. I could have shown a third box as a dependent schedule thread ("Integration Set 1 Thread") to show this but chose not to for simplicity of presentation.

There are several points to be made about this segment of the schedule:

■ To provide a big-picture view, I purposely used single boxes to represent units D and E schedule threads rather than clutter up this figure.
■ You can't do the "create/update integration test" activity until all elements of integration set 2 are "done." The integration plan specified all this.
■ The object specified in the integration-type activities is "Integration Set 2." This should exactly match what was specified in the integration plan. Also, the schedule reader will get a visual insight into the integration plan by clearly showing that units D and E are indeed integration set 2.

I will now deal with unit F. I will repeat here what we know about unit F:

■ It is to be totally designed and implemented.
■ It does not need to be unit tested.
■ It is the only part of the third integration set.

Based on that information, our schedule thread for unit F now looks like Figure 6.11.

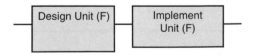

Figure 6.11   Unit F schedule thread.

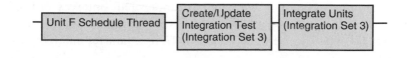

Figure 6.12   Integration set 3 schedule thread.

Please note the following about this portion of the schedule related to unit F (Figure 6.1):

- I've added "(F)" to the schedule instance to bind the activity to the object (in this case, "unit F") for this graphical depiction.
- There is no unit test or test driver activity needed — just the design and implementation.
- Integration set 3 requires:
  - Both integration sets 1 and 2 to be completed
  - Unit F thread to be complete

When unit F gets implemented, you will be able to place the third integration-type activity on the schedule as shown in Figure 6.12.

It is important to note that you can't integrate set 3 until integration sets 1 and 2 have been integrated and tested. I could have shown these integration threads as dependent schedule threads but chose not to for simplicity of presentation.

I am hoping that you now clearly get the connection of schedule tasks to process activities *and* the connection from activities to schedule tasks. You should have a one-to-one relationship of schedule task instances to process activities. The schedule predecessor/successor relationships should be exactly the same as depicted in the end-to-end life-cycle story of activities. You should be able to morph the end-to-end life-cycle process story to the project schedule and vice versa. *This is the essence of connecting processes to the real world in this software process model approach.*

Activities

The collective set of activities is located in the second layer of the process pyramid. I will be using the term "activity" throughout this book because that term is appropriate for the "what you have to do" process elements. At two different divisions of the same company, process elements were called standard practices and operating procedures. Of these terms, I really objected to "operating procedures" but was overridden by a vice president who had no clue about processes. We call this the repeatable level because activities are "what you have to do" — not "how you are to do it." In this software process model, we may have more than one way of fulfilling a how-to due to scaling, tool variations, site variations, etc. — but we have a single "what" to be done to get that important repeatability aspect addressed.

The activity is the major aspect of this process model and for that reason I will address this part of the process model right now before dealing with other layers of the pyramid model.

There are several rules for determining whether something qualifies as an activity:

- Is it schedulable? Can it be placed on a schedule with predetermined successors/predecessors?
- Can a verb or object form describe it? Is it a self-contained action?
- Can it be described with a set of high-level steps? If there are any if-then-else connotations, you are too low!
- Can you place an instance of this on a schedule with different objects on which to execute? That is, can you place multiple versions of this (same verb) on a schedule with different objects involved?
- Can your life cycle be expressed by a set of activities? This is where you achieve repeatability at the activity level.
- Can you identify a small set of high-level "what" steps for the activity? This is where you achieve repeatability within an activity.
- Does it produce one or more work products to signify that it is "done"?
- Can it be selected in total or not? Is it the lowest selectable process element at the "what you do" level?

The heart of determining what that activity set is starts with schedule analysis and lead interviews.

By merely analyzing schedules, you can quickly determine a get-started set of activities. This effort takes all the variations to the theme for schedules and condenses them down to a pick list of process activities. In software engineering environments, this pick list of activities tends to be about 40 items for all scheduled activities or tasks. The resultant set reflects the engineering tasks to be done.

My experience with schedule development indicates a total free-for-all in the way traditional schedules get developed. Some task items are noun-based, some are verb-based, some describe the same thing differently (based on who submitted it), and, finally, the level of detail is all over the map. We want to get total consistency for schedules and, at the same time, directly tie the real work of schedules to the process world.

Once a proposed set of activities is developed, simply ask the leads about:

- Inputs and outputs to address the key data drivers
- Predecessor/successor relationships to other activities

I've had some interviews where separate leads have given me dissimilar inputs and outputs for the same activity! When you run into this problem, you are looking at embedded process problems that will need sorting out. A worse process problem can surface if you are told that any particular input can be obtained from one of several work products. This raises the question of what input source to trust. The leads will readily tell you that you can't execute this kind of activity until some other activity (or set of activities) terminates. Again, if you get differing answers about the same activity, you have a process problem to sort out. The goal is to end up with a set of activities that can be connected to one another (called the "end-to-end life cycle") and whose inputs and outputs are clearly defined.

If, after this analysis, you end up with designated inputs and outputs that are just there (i.e., no connectivity to anything), you have a serious process problem to sort out before going much further. Over time, company processes can reach this abnormal state.

I used the simple form shown in Figure 6.13 to fill out with lead interviews to get this kind of data.

Once defined, you should be able to "morph" the end-to-end life cycle of the process world onto activity instances as shown on project schedules — and vice versa. If you do this right, you should be able to take a project schedule and condense activity instances to single-instance views and recreate the end-to-end process life-cycle story. Conversely, you should be able to take the end-to-end process life-cycle story and create

ACTIVITY	
INPUTS	OUTPUTS

Figure 6.13   Activity analysis form.

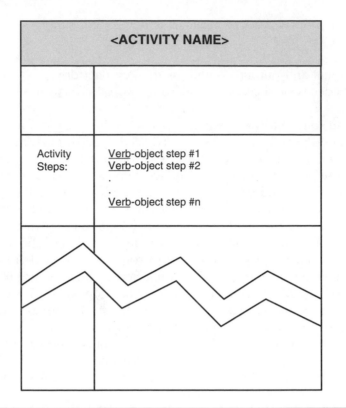

Figure 6.14 Tabular format.

project schedules with differing instances of each activity. Then you have a powerful real-world connection of processes to schedules. You no longer have the notion that processes are over there and scheduling tasking is over here. The "here" and "there" are one and the same thing.

From an implementation perspective, I have represented the activity as both a simple table format and a graphical step-based format. The biggest difference in format presentation is in the way high-level steps are presented. The table format in Figure 6.14 shows the high-level steps embedded in that table. The graphical format in Figure 6.15 shows the high-level steps as separate graphical entities.

In an earlier implementation, we went to elaborate lengths to connect the steps with various forms of arrows to indicate such things as:

■ Must follow prior step
■ Can overlap prior step
■ Can be concurrent with prior step

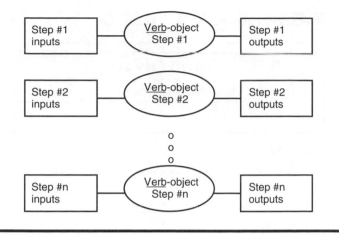

Figure 6.15   Graphical format.

In a later implementation, we merely asserted that if the inputs were there, you could do the step! That was much simpler. This input presence assertion became the later rule for high-level steps no matter which representation was presented. In both representations, you hyperlink off the verb for those high-level steps that have a how-to (procedure or work instruction) elaboration. The hyperlink goes to the "how selector," which will be described later. Those verbs not hyperlinked represent high-level "what" steps with no how-to process elements. Again, not all "whats" need a "how." Every "how" does need a "what," however.

For this book, I will use the tabular form for simplicity. However, the graphical-based representation has a tighter level of work-product granularity at each high-level "what you have to do" step that, for some companies, is too detailed. The tabular form deals with activity work products at the activity level and does not have tight connectivity and data flows for each step. The tabular form had an unexpected surprise in that you could create a very simple HTML format that could be modified by any standard Word application. Word allows "save as HTML" as one of the "save as" options. This really opened up the number of people who could maintain this process model.

Figure 6.16 shows what an activity looks like. The figure will be the basis of discussion for the rest of the chapter.

The text shown in this figure is constant text (i.e., use "as is"). You personalize the yellow-filled boxes and the right column for each activity. The intent is to have an activity representation that:

- Will fit on a single Web page for the most part
- Will be simple to read and maintain

Predecessor Activities:	Successor Activities:

<ACTIVITY NAME> 2005/10/01	
(Generic Object Name)	
Activity Description:	
Activity Dependencies:	
Activity Inputs:	
Activity Steps:	
Activity Outputs:	
Activity Metrics:	
Activity Training:	
Activity Group:	
Activity Roles:	
How Selectors Used by This Activity:	
Activity Estimations:	

Figure 6.16   Activity format.

Once at the actual activity, you now have a one-stop shopping display of all the pertinent information you need to execute that schedule task instance. I will describe the activity informational topics as two lists: mandatory activity topics and possible extension activity topics.

Mandatory Activity Topics

Predecessor/Successor Activities

This is shown "outside" the activity to indicate which activity comes before this activity (predecessor links) and which activity comes after this activity (successor links). You can traverse activities in a horizontal fashion across the end-to-end life cycle when these activity references are hyperlinks to other activities.

Activity Name

You place the activity name here along with its generic object name at the very top to clearly identify the activity. You could attach a date to the name so that the reader will identify the version of this process element. In this software process model, the term "version" is strictly by date. You will notice that I've used the European way of displaying the date (year, month, and day) on purpose. I am setting this up for script processing to pull out the HTML tag for date to establish the process basis for any project. With a single tagged date field in all the process elements, I only need a single start date on any project to select all the project elements that are candidates for that project's process basis. The date equal to or closest to that start date is part of the process basis for that project. The HTML-tagged date field is important throughout this model. I am describing just the activity date field here. Because activities are all candidates for use, all activities are part of the process basis for any project.

Activity Description

This is a short description of what this activity is all about. Some companies may want to have a "more" hyperlink added to the end here to get verbose about what this activity is all about outside this Web page. I cannot overemphasize that the main description is a short summary-type of description. I like to keep this to a single line with the "more" hyperlink. The intent is to encapsulate this activity on a single Web page if at all possible.

Activity Dependencies

This is your chance to identify external dependencies — beyond precursor activity execution. Examples might involve a test type of activity that has a dependency of a test lab environment being set up and in place. All activities have dependencies on having input work products being "there" and ready to use. This field is geared to dependencies beyond the explicit process-based dependencies.

Activity Inputs

All work product inputs are shown here. The line items must be outputs from some other activity. It is acceptable to use generic terms here if there are variations of any work product. On one implementation, I showed the hyperlinked name (or names) of the activities in parentheses following the work product name to clearly identify where any input came from. Users found this helpful.

Activity Steps

This is a short list of high-level steps that are in a verb/object form of "what has to be done." The steps are the heart of any activity. Although shown in a linear fashion, any step can be executed if its inputs are there. This rule allows for concurrency at the step level. This is where we connect the high-level "what" steps (via each verb) to the how selectors — for those "whats" that require a "how." There are two rules to be a high-level step. It must be:

- Something that you absolutely, positively want done (somehow).
- A "what" anchor to an important how-to process element. Configuration management–type operations are examples of this in a software engineering environment. This is where you get a link to important configuration management (CM) procedures for control of those work products. You want them mandated as high-level steps. Depending on the work product, you can perform formal CM or informal developmental CM via this mechanism.

There are certain high-level steps that exist in all activities as part of this model. These steps are as follows:

- "Begin" step. This hyperlinked verb is executed by the activity lead and is intended to inform the activity team what charge numbers are involved for this schedule task (if applicable). The activity lead (or responsible person) may also use this mechanism to notify people like the project manager or development manager that this activity has started. If your company has no need for charge number assignments or to let anyone know that an activity is starting, you may delete this step.

- "Get" step. This hyperlinked verb is there as an anchor to support an important CM procedural how-to. The activity team members use this step. This is a great place to hook your mandated what-you-have-to-do world to your CM system. If your inputs are informal work products, you would direct the process practitioner to the CM how-to process element to "get" what the practioner wants from that developmental repository — using whatever CM tool is involved.

- "Inspect" step. This hyperlinked verb is there to mandate inspections on all work products prior to hand-off. The work product leads and designated inspectors use this step. A key aspect of this process model is that we place the monkey on the producer's back for quality prior to passing it on to the next activity in the life cycle. A lot of companies seem to have the opposite philosophy on pass-off as being a "good luck to you" attitude. The "inspect" step is our quality gate within each activity and it gets us to the inspection how-to process element.

- "Put" step. This hyperlinked verb is there as an anchor to support an important CM procedural how-to. The activity team members use this step. If your outputs are informal work products, you would direct the process practitioner to the CM how-to process element to "put" what has been inspected into the developmental repository — using whatever CM tool is involved. If the work product requires a more formal CM method, then we will point the practitioner to a more formal CM how-to process element.

- "End" step. This hyperlinked verb is executed by the activity lead and is intended to notify people like the project manager, development manager, schedulers (for earned value), activity team members (for ending time charges), estimators (to collect actuals), and the next activity lead that this activity has ended. The hyperlinked verb "notify" is also there to support metrics data hand-off by the activity lead to whatever group gets this data. For "Design Down" activities, this is where you notify SCM to expand the SCM developmental repository and accounting to expand your project's charge numbers. This step is essential to this model.

I have suggested the above list of verbs. Each company that implements this process model may choose alternative verbs that are more suitable to their culture. Some companies use "evaluate" versus "inspect," for example. I do recommend that these steps exist in some form.

I have found it useful to associate a role with each and every step. On one implementation, the roles were encapsulated in square brackets for each high-level step. This opens the door to having a script go through all the process activities to generate any role-to-activity matrix. It also opens the door to clearly specify what each role is expected to do. Can you imagine what this can do for employee promotions when training can be clearly identified for each role? All this comes from this software process model.

Activity Outputs

All the work product outputs are shown here. It is important to hyperlink each and every output to the work product set (described later in the support layer). Each work product set includes:

- Work product template
- Work product inspection checklist
- Work product guideline (optional)
- Work product example(s) (optional)

Think about it — wouldn't it be great to point a developer-author to all this if we're asking someone to create any work product! I found that the practitioners loved this aspect of the software process model as it "holds their hand" and allows them to concentrate on the reasons why they were hired. The mentioned work products must be inputs to some other activity. It is acceptable to use generic terms here if there are variations of any work product. On one implementation, I showed the hyperlinked name (or names) of the activities in parentheses following the work product name to clearly identify where any output went.

Activity Metrics

Identify what metrics are involved with this activity execution. Per the roles above, it opens the door to having a script go through all the process activities to generate any metrics-to-activity matrix. For metrics, it's important to note that those activities marked for metrics just collect metrics data. They do not convert metrics data to useful information. Any metrics data is passed to whatever group is designated to receive metrics data via the "End" step in all activities. If you find it complicated to gather metrics data, this is a great place to hyperlink to the data collection procedural how-to.

Activity Training

In order to execute this activity, are there any special training requirements needed for success? These are specialized training requirements beyond hire expertise. For example, a design-type activity may require the designer to have specialized requirements database tool training to deal with allocated requirements coming out of the design. This is part of the software process model that directly addresses training needs to process activities, which in turn identifies training needs to execute schedule tasks successfully! This also opens the door to have a script to create a training-needs matrix by activity or by role.

Possible Extension Activity Topics

Activity Group

This binds a particular activity to a preset list of umbrella terms used for project management metrics and project estimations. This will work if an individual activity is associated with one and only one activity group. If you want to create a pie chart showing the percentage of time spent on things like requirements analysis, design, coding, engineering testing, system testing, etc., then relate each and every activity to one of these topics. You should be able to map one or more activities to an activity group. If you wanted to capture efforts involved in unit testing, then "Create/Update Unit Test" and "Test Unit" would be marked with the same activity group as unit testing. You can achieve this same mapping outside this process element and will need to do this mapping externally if any activity belongs to more than one activity group. Once executed as an instance on a schedule, you can capture actuals and add it to that activity group "bin" of effort. You can actually compare your life-cycle percentages with industry norms using this feature.

Activity Roles

Show all the roles involved in the execution of this activity as a one-stop shopping list. This information is also used to produce the roles matrix later on. It is important to use role names and not titles, because roles tend to be static whereas titles come and go with each reorganization. This same information can be gleaned from each and every step if you choose not to summarize roles at the activity level. Some found it useful to summarize this here even though it was a potential maintenance issue if this summarized list did not keep in synch with the roles specified per step.

How Selectors Are Used by the Activity

This option provides a quick summary of all the procedures (via their how selectors) used by this activity. This can be deduced by the hyperlink destinations of the verb-based hyperlinks in the high-level steps. For some implementations, that might suffice. Like summarized activity roles, this could be a maintenance problem if this list did not agree with those in the steps. This opens the door to a script to create a how selector usage matrix by activity.

Activity Estimations

On one implementation, I found it useful to provide a place where actuals are captured from history to assist the planners in the future to estimate activity efforts. Although not absolutely essential, you may agree with me that this is useful. At one company, we ended up with a hyperlinked "container" document per subsystem where each subsystem lead could retain useful (and real) information to assist in future estimations.

Activities in General

Now that we have explained each activity field in great detail, there are some comments that need to be made about each activity:

- Tasks are placed on a project schedule from a predetermined set of process activities. This provides the real-world connection to processes. At one place where I worked, we placed the set of process activity names right on the project schedule template. Each process activity name was hyperlinked right to the activity Web page. Setting up a project schedule became a select-and-copy operation (with a mouse) to set up each schedule task. This way, each schedule task was directly hyperlinked to the process activity that described exactly what had to be done.
- Predecessor/successor rules on a project schedule come directly from the end-to-end life-cycle process story. This is another key aspect of this software process model method. The contents of each PAD gave incredible guidance to anyone setting up a project schedule.

- The activity is designed to be totally auditable. High-level steps can be validated. Inspections can be validated. Notifications can be validated. Metrics can be validated. Auditing can be done by anyone — not just by quality personnel. Auditing can be performed offline (and after the fact) so that there is no auditing impact! This is another key aspect of this software process method. Auditing can be done by anyone in line with the ISO 9001 notion of "quality is everyone's responsibility" and it's totally noninvasive. You can achieve this without impacting the main development effort! You can even make this auditing function close to real time and make it an integral part of your "End" high-level step to ensure process compliance before going to the next activity as yet another aspect of being done. The software process method is that flexible in this area.

- You don't place an instance of an activity on a schedule unless you know for sure that it is to be executed. I distinguish between schedule planning packages and schedule work packages. Planning packages are best-guess estimates for what needs to be done in whatever granularity is appropriate. Once you get better visibility, you convert planning packages to work packages. It is the work package that is the activity instance. These are the schedule tasks that need to be executed. It is the work package that is the basis for earned value calculations. The term "work package" is synonymous with the term "schedule task," which is synonymous with a "process activity instance." The software process method absolutely aligns the process world with the real world of schedules.

- Although an activity can be selected for an instance execution on a project schedule, you can also choose not to have an activity instance on a schedule. Selection granularity is at the activity level. This is an important aspect of the software process method. The activity itself is selectable based on your designs and plans.

- Once selected, *all* the high-level steps in an activity are required to be complete as part of schedule execution. This gives total repeatability at each activity level. This is a powerful concept built into the software process model approach. This ensures that each and every activity instance on a schedule of the same process activity in the process world has absolute repeatability.

- Execution of some activities provides that extended visibility for further activity instances. For example, higher-level design types of activities not only design to the next lower level of decomposition but also provide real insight into what and how many certain follow-on activities should be placed on the schedule. The same is true of activities that generate plans. *(I have determined that the integration plan is probably the most important plan for this emerging activity instance schedule formation.)* These are examples where some activity executions perform a dual role: one as part of the target life cycle and one as a process activity schedule instance selector. The software process model approach recognizes this duality and reinforces the value of good designs and plans.

■ Each high-level step in an activity is not bound by similar weighting. Some high-level steps are trivial steps and some are not. All steps are to be executed by the role (or roles) designated for that step.

By breaking the entire life cycle down into phase-based chunks called PADs that in turn contain executable elements called "activities," we can instantiate these activities on a project schedule, thus connecting processes to the real world. Work products are directly connected to activities. You execute an activity instance (or task), and you get one or more work products associated with that activity. Because of this mapping, you can relate work product production with activity instance execution on a project schedule. This work product/activity connection allows this software process model approach to work directly with any work product–based tools that have low-level processes per work product production cycle. These tools quite often have built-in promotion/demotion processes to reflect a mini–life cycle for any given work product. This process approach is not at odds with these tools.

The activity is thus the centerpiece of this software process model. Let's turn our attention to the how-to world in the next section.

Chapter 7

Side 1 — Level 3 Implementation Level

How Selectors

How selectors are intermediate Web pages between the activity's high-level step verbs and the how-to procedures. How selectors also exist for asynchronous event-based procedures. In general, I do not allow a direct reference to any how-to procedure without going through a how selector. This is the software process model mechanism where we achieve extensibility and flexibility at the how-to level. Procedural how-to process elements require a "what" to exist. The "what" options can be:

- Any high-level "what" step verb inside an activity that has a how-to connection.
- A high-level "what" requirement in the authority level. These can be company policy requirements, ISO 9001 requirements, regulatory requirements, or maturity model goals and practices. These reflect a direct how-to solution to that high-level "what."
- An implied "what" based on the nature of your business, accepted business norms, or standard engineering practices. These reflect a direct how-to solution to aspects of your business that have no explicit "what."

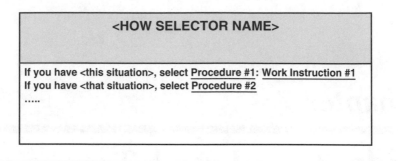

Figure 7.1   How selector format.

If you feel the need to write a how-to process element (procedure or work instruction), where's the "what" requirement that is its reason for being? Another way of saying this is that every "how" requires a "what" but not every "what" requires one or more "how-tos." To illustrate this point, I will now show (see Figure 7.1) what one of these how selectors would look like as an example.

Figure 7.1 shows that procedure #1 has a corresponding work instruction whereas procedure #2 does not. This model encourages a short mind-jogger single Web page presentation as the procedure with a side link to its more verbose and detailed work instruction. The work instructions give you an excruciating level of detail whereas the procedure does not. You could skip the procedure and go right to the verbose and detailed work instruction. It has been my experience that process users don't take too well to poring over pages and pages of process stuff to get to what they want. Take my advice and have both how-to elements to satisfy the experienced process user and the novice process user where it makes sense to do so. They will love you for it.

You get to these how selectors from the following "what" places:

- Hyperlinked high-level requirements found in company policies. This is how you connect policy statements with how-to procedures.
- A hyperlinked verb in any high-level step within an activity that requires a how-to elaboration. This is how you connect "what you have to do" steps inside any activity with "how you are to do it" procedures.
- A hyperlinked reference from international standards (e.g., an ISO 9001 requirement). Each ISO 9001 requirement is a high-level "what." The ISO 9001 requirement that states, "The supplier shall have a corrective action system" can serve as the high-level "what" to connect to the "corrective action" how selector. This connectivity can be directly shown to any ISO 9001 auditor in the ISO 9001

compliance matrix. I recommend directly placing a hyperlink on the "shall" verb right to the appropriate how selector.

■ A hyperlinked reference from government regulations (e.g., FAA/FDA regulations). Each regulation is a high-level "what" to connect to the how selector that answers the regulatory mail. This connectivity can be directly shown to any government auditor for compliance. It is important to connect the regulatory verb to the appropriate how selector.

In addition to these connections, we need traversal and accessibility ease on the Web. For that reason, we can also get to how selectors by:

■ A how selector list accessed via a hyperlink button on all process Web pages
■ A how selector summarized list within an activity — if you choose to have this optional field

In the body of the how selector, you specify the selection criteria to select any of the how-to procedural elements. The selection criteria can be:

■ *Project specific.* "If it is project ABC, select <u>Procedure #1</u>. If it is project DEF, select <u>Procedure #2</u>: <u>Work Instruction #2</u>." You would use these selection criteria when tool sets are different or when one project has "a better mousetrap." One has just a procedure and one has a two-layered how-to as a procedure and corresponding work instruction.
■ *Site specific.* "If San Diego projects, select <u>Procedure #1</u>. If Dallas projects, select <u>Procedure #2</u>: <u>Work Instruction #2</u>." Typically, sites do have variances in tools and almost certainly will on business acquisitions. This process model handles this very nicely.
■ *Scope specific.* "For internal company projects, select <u>Procedure #1</u>. For external projects, select <u>Work Instruction #2</u>." Internal projects may not need the same rigor as external projects.
■ *Tool specific.* "For tool ABC, use <u>Procedure #1</u>. For tool DEF, use <u>Procedure #2</u>: <u>Work Instruction #2</u>."
■ *Scale specific.* "For small projects (less than six months), select <u>Procedure #1</u>. For medium projects (six months through two years), select <u>Procedure #2</u>. For large projects (more than two years), select <u>Procedure #3</u>: <u>Work Instruction #3</u>." These selection criteria recognize that shorter-duration projects do things differently than longer-duration projects.

■ *Specific.* "The only selection allowed is <u>Procedure #1</u>: <u>Work Instruction #1</u>." This is where the organization wants one and only one way of performing the how-to procedure. It clearly states that alternative selections are not allowed.

The underlined portions above represent hyperlinks to that designated procedure or work instruction.

In all instances, the how selector exists as a front end to its procedure/work instruction selection set. Even if there is one and only one how-to option, the how selector still exists and states the one selection. For my implementations, I have insisted on having a how selector — even for a single selection. This was done for process consistency, recognizing that a slight indirection is not a big deal for process selection. Over time, when you have variations at the how-to level to add, this is where you get to add that new procedural how-to approach. If you get a "better mousetrap" procedural element, you merely add it as an additional option in the how selector. This is how you accomplish flexibility and extensibility at the how-to procedural level.

The how selector is the mechanism to produce procedural tailoring. You tailor by selection rather than by modifying that one-size-fits-all procedural element. An important notion of this software process model is that procedural tailoring is done by selection — not by corrupting any one-size-fits-all procedure to force it to fit all your situations.

An interesting side issue occurs by allowing different how-to solutions to use this how selector approach: Good procedural elements survive naturally whereas bad ones die naturally. As a process guy, I can easily set up usage counters on Web sites to get a handle on which ones are truly used and which ones aren't! If you're seeing that option #1 is used 10,000 times and option #2 is used six times, it's probably an indicator that option #1 is good whereas option #2 is bad.

The directional flow is from the how selector to the procedural how-to elements. This software process model disallows any reverse directional flow. The rationale for this is simple: Once at a procedure selection, you know where you are and you can always get back to the how selector via the standard Web "back" capability. I do allow a hyperlink from the one-page procedure to a more detailed work instruction as a lateral link for Web usability. This last link connects any procedure with its work instruction counterpart.

We will now look at the wonderful world of procedural how-to elements. This is where "the rubber meets the road" for process practitioners.

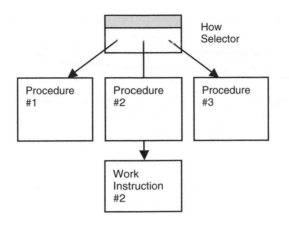

Figure 7.2 Connecting how-tos to a how selector.

Procedures

A procedure is also a how-to process element suitable for your experienced process user. If you feel the need to write any procedural element, ask where the "what" is. If you can't answer that question, get rid of your urge!

In this software process model, a procedure is a how-to process element that is directly connected to a how selector Web page. You can have 1…n procedure options (or selections) per how selector. This looks like Figure 7.2.

Any and all variations of a procedural how-to (via the how selector) are elaborations of one or more of the following "what" items:

- High-level "what" step (verb) within an activity
- High-level "what" requirement of an international standard (e.g., ISO 9001)
- High-level "what" compliance of a maturity model (e.g., CMMI)
- High-level "what" compliance of a government regulation (e.g., FDA regulation)
- Any implied "what" compliance to your type of business
- Any "what" compliance from an asynchronous event-driven stimulus

Every how selector should map to one or more of the above anchors. For example, "the supplier shall have a corrective action system" is an ISO 9001 requirement. This is an example of a high-level "what" anchor (in the authority level) that connects to a how selector — for one or more variations of any "corrective action" procedure (in the implementation level).

You don't need a how-to procedure for all "whats." Having said this, a procedure can be:

- A simple checklist of mind-jogger things to do
- A simple flowchart
- A combination of text and flow to convey how things are to be done

In this software process model, a procedure is an elaboration of a "what." Don't call something a procedure if it doesn't satisfy that basic understanding.

I would stay away from embedding names or titles in any process element — especially a procedure. That guarantees a maintenance problem. I would also stay away from linking a procedure to lower-level procedures. Consider the procedure as the lowest "leaf" of the process tree. I would not make this more complex than it needs to be.

The procedure is an important process element to connect work products and forms to support the how-to. References to work products and forms hyperlink from the procedure (in the implementation level) to the work product and form sets (in the support level). Tools and tool variations show up in the procedural how-to level. These tool variations are addressed directly in the procedural selections. In one implementation, we used a product called LiveLink for document version control and used ClearCase for software version control. You might see something like the following in the how selector to address this as a tool-specific selection criterion:

- For LiveLink, use <u>procedure #1</u>
- For ClearCase, use <u>procedure #2</u>

This way, we directly address tool variations in performing version control.

It is desirable to have a standard header format that states that it really is a procedure and has a date stamp as a version. Standard header things like page counts are also desirable. Like other process elements, procedures should be HTML elements such that the HTML date tag can be used intelligently to determine which procedural versions apply to any project. I am not big on complex (and long) headers. Keep in mind that these procedures are primarily viewed on a computer screen via the Web. Don't squander valuable screen space with headers. Keep it short. Companies that come from a paper document culture tend to forget that we only print things out for reference and the real usage is via the display mode on-screen.

There is one particular procedure that is critical to the success of this software process model: *the inspection procedure*. Because this process model has built-in inspections within all activities, it becomes crucial that this particular procedure is efficient and has broad buy-in by the practitioners. This particular procedure has a tight coupling with the inspection checklist described later in the support level. Make this as simple as possible out of the box and get people to really use it first before any embellishments are made. On one successful implementation, I created an inspection procedure that had these characteristics:

- An intranet-based tool where findings were entered online and accessible to all employees (local or remote). All inspectors could see all findings, and there is a total auditable database of inspections performed, when performed, against what work products, for which activity, and who participated.
- Three roles only were defined: work product lead, work product author, and work product inspector.
- Based on the fundamental FAGAN defect focus on the inspection meeting (i.e., the meeting dealt with defects and not solutions).
- Redlines covered by a single finding, "redlines as noted," with details passed back to the author for resolution. These redlines can really be redlines or "track changes" for a document. This is done to ensure real findings get covered at the meeting while the author does all the minute stuff offline.
- Activity work products predefined for process metrics. I allowed free-form data entry of work product type beyond the standard set. With a drop-down list of predetermined work products, you can get some marvelous inspection defect metrics by work product and by activity.
- Findings became the inspection meeting agenda (i.e., if you don't submit a finding, you don't get to discuss things at the meeting).
- Meeting participation and availability used standard Microsoft Outlook.
- Disagreement findings were handled first at the meeting, followed by discussion findings, followed by agreed-to findings. This results in short, cost-effective meetings.
- Automatic tool notification to the inspectors provided the URL for finding submissions.
- Automatic e-mail notification to author on submitted findings.

■ Automatic email notification back to inspector when author did not agree with finding. This allowed one-on-one resolution prior to inspection meeting.

■ Finding tied to activity in the end-to-end life cycle for process metrics on where defect was really caught.

■ Finding tied to suggested activity in the end-to-end life cycle for defect prevention (i.e., where it should have been caught).

■ No inspection meeting when author totally agreed with all findings (i.e., no wasted time on pre-agreed items). I realize that there is value in the "invisible inspector" to have a real meeting and that group dynamics can indeed create additional findings beyond any inspector's inputs. In the commercial environment at the time, the tight schedules had precedence.

■ Built-in quick-press reports to get all findings for any given inspection (i.e., this is used as the common sheet of music that all meeting participants work from).

■ Emphasis on author/lead to process the findings with no verification. This not only saves time but also squarely places the monkey on the lead's back to make sure that all findings were addressed before marking "done."

■ Optionally, add inspection metrics at the end as to how long the inspection itself took, etc., in hours. The work product lead fills this in.

When implementing this process framework architecture, this particular procedure deserves high priority.

Having discussed procedures, let's now look at the supporting process players: the work products and forms.

Chapter 8

Side 1 — Level 4 Support Level

Work Products

It should be intuitively obvious by now that if you break down your life cycle into schedulable activities, develop a set of procedures that elaborate on those activity steps, fill in procedural holes beyond that to satisfy authority-level things (policies, ISO 9001, CMMI goals and activities, regulations), and fill in procedural holes for asynchronous event-driven tasks, you not only will have a complete process set but you'll also have a defined set of work products for your complete process support!

What are work products? These could be Word documents, PowerPoint presentations, Excel spreadsheets, source code, XML figures, UML diagrams, VISIO charts, requirements databases, etc.

With this software process model, you should be able to take any work product and identify:

- Which activity (at the repeatable level) created, used, or updated it
- Which procedure (at the implementation level) created, used, or updated it

Anyone using this software process model method should be able to create a work product–centric matrix that provides that story.

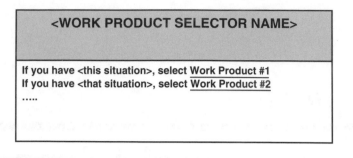

Figure 8.1 Work product selector format.

This software process model tightly couples work products with activities. You can't declare any activity "done" until all the work products associated with that activity are inspected and placed under configuration management (CM) control. The sheer presence of any inspected and controlled work product is one piece of auditable evidence that the activity was indeed "done."

I realized a long time ago that when you talk about a "work product" you really have:

- Variations of work products consistent with how-to variances.
- An associative set of things that collectively go with each work product. I call this group of things the "work product set."

To address work product variances, this process model has a similar method to the how selector, called a work product selector. This provides the needed flexibility and extensibility at the work product level by selecting the appropriate work product. A work product selector looks like Figure 8.1.

You will find this particularly useful when you really want work product variances to provide work products in a single class.

Once at a particular work product, the work product set is composed of the following:

- The work product template
- The work product inspection checklist
- The work product guidelines
- The work product example(s)

The first two bullet items should always be there (*initially, you'll have template and inspection checklist holes until your process repository becomes more robust*). The last two bullet items tend to be optional. I found that examples, however, are a great way to shorten time to market and rapidly get up on deliverable expectations. I don't know about you but I learn more from an example than anything else. This software process model recognizes this and flaunts it by building it into the selectable process elements.

You get to a work product set:

- From a hyperlinked work product reference within activities or procedures
- From a Web page reference to a list of work product sets — which in turn hyperlinks to any particular work product set

The work product set is an important concept. You will find that changes to a work product template invariably change other members of the set. For example, a template change could affect the inspection checklist, optional guidelines, and posted examples. A lesser effect is when you update the inspection checklist to make it more complete without impacting other members of the set. I have seen software leads compete to place their best work products into the process repository. The human side of this encouraged high-quality examples and pride of ownership.

Work Product Template

For a lot of tools, there is no need for a template because the template is tool-generated. For example, if you use Rational Rose and Unified Modeling Language (UML), the nine diagrams (work products) are created by the tool; therefore, there is no need for a template.

For non-tool work products, this first member of the work product set is absolutely essential to the success of your process execution. Think about it — if you ask someone to produce a document called a software design document (SDD), the first question is "what is it?" before you get started. A template can rapidly provide that answer and provide a framework in which you can add documentation "meat" to the template "bones." Having been a software programmer for many years and subsequently working with software engineers, I know that anything you can do to help them with getting a deliverable out will make you a friend of the troops.

The intent of the template within the support level is to:

- Deal with the entire formatting overhead *once* offline for consistency with other company deliverables.
- Provide a table of contents and structure to be followed.
- Provide all boilerplate text including legal and contractual wording.

I can tell you from firsthand experience that software engineers don't create templates well. They are typically not English majors and sometimes English may not be their first language! A template gets all the extraneous (but important) stuff done and is ready to go to achieve work product consistency by your process practitioners. This separation of skills is important to this process model. Software engineers should concentrate on the computer science stuff — not header and footer formats, cover pages, revision pages, etc. Leave that work to your technical editors.

Work Product Inspection Checklist

This second member of the work product set is also essential to the success of your process execution. This process model insists on built-in inspections of most work products prior to handing them off to the next person or group in the end-to-end life cycle. I say "most" because not all work products are created equal. Some definitely need to be inspected prior to handoff (e.g., a design work product) whereas some don't (e.g., status report work product). If there's any doubt, inspect.

This is to place the monkey on the producer's back rather than to pass stuff off to the next fellow with a "good luck to you" mentality! These built-in inspections are quality gates for produced work products. With inspections, you can achieve better quality at all links in the end-to-end life-cycle chain. This also supports the notion that earlier inspections eliminate defects being found at the back end of the life cycle. We want higher inspection findings (which are cheap) rather than higher problem reports at system testing time (which are expensive) or customer-found problems (which are astronomical and could cost you your business).

Having said all this, your company's inspection procedure itself could make or break this process model. I have personally seen horrible examples of this. I am a big believer in tailoring this particular procedure to the process maturity of the organization. This is similar to talking to children at an age-appropriate level. One company tried a full-blown FAGAN inspection technique for an organization that was barely paper trained in process. It didn't go over at all — even though the FAGAN approach is very good. You are far better off at a "subcompact" level of procedure rather than a "luxury" version out of the box. You can improve your procedure naturally over time to better meet the increasing maturity level of the organization. I have been guilty of saying "that's a great idea" to someone who has suggested a more robust procedure — even though I felt we should have been there all along! It's amazing how much better processes get followed when it comes from "them" versus "you." Your customer's comments count a lot. It's also in keeping with basic Six Sigma concepts of making sure you understand your customer's needs.

These procedures may be called "inspection procedures," "evaluation procedures," or "review procedures." At this point, I want to get on a soapbox about a fundamental difference between the terms "inspection" and "review."

- The point of an inspection is to find defects.
- The point of a review is to externalize your target work product to a group of people (for educational purposes), and you *might* uncover defects as a secondary consideration.

In the DoD contracting world, they talk about SRRs (software requirements reviews), PDRs (preliminary design reviews), and CDRs (critical design reviews). They all externalize the target of the review to an audience. You *may* find defects — but that's not the main objective of the review.

We want inspections within each activity. We want to dig out defects at each and every task in the end-to-end life cycle. We also want to address both defect detection and defect prevention. Defect detection happens at each and every inspection. Defect prevention occurs at (or after) each and every inspection when we consciously ask, "Where *should* these defects have been found" in the activity end-to-end life cycle? On one implementation of an inspection procedure, I had a pull-down list of activities for just that purpose. I asked inspectors, authors, and leads to take a shot at where they thought these defects should have been found. The process group took this as input and used that information as a feedback loop to upgrade inspection checklists in earlier activities. We used the inspection checklist itself as the mechanism to constantly improve quality at the activity places where they *should* be picked up! This way, we kept improving earlier inspection quality and reduced findings in later inspections. This software process model approach directly addresses continuous process improvement through this mechanism.

The problem I've run into is an "inspect-this" kind of handoff. How many of you have been thrown a document and told to review it? This open-ended assignment is an open invitation to:

- Misuse people's expertise
- Waste time
- Encourage formatting-only findings

The inspection checklist organization coupled with the inspection procedure can eliminate all this.

```
┌─────────────────────────────────────────┐
│  ┌───────────────────────────────────┐  │
│  │      INSPECTION CHECKLIST for      │  │
│  │         <WORK PRODUCT>             │  │
│  │                                   │  │
│  └───────────────────────────────────┘  │
│  ┌───────────────────────────────────┐  │
│  │  Suggested Roles Criteria:         │  │
│  │                                   │  │
│  ├───────────────────────────────────┤  │
│  │  Entry Criteria (Author):          │  │
│  │                                   │  │
│  ├───────────────────────────────────┤  │
│  │  Inspection Criteria (<Role A>):   │  │
│  │  ┌─────────────────────────────┐   │  │
│  │  │                             │   │  │
│  │  │                             │   │  │
│  │  └─────────────────────────────┘   │  │
│  │  Inspection Criteria (<Role B>):   │  │
│  │  ┌─────────────────────────────┐   │  │
│  │  │                             │   │  │
│  │  │                             │   │  │
│  │  └─────────────────────────────┘   │  │
│  └───────────────────────────────────┘  │
└─────────────────────────────────────────┘
```

Figure 8.2   Inspection checklist format.

Having said all this, let's turn our attention to the inspection checklist itself. See Figure 8.2 for an inspection checklist format.

Here's a breakdown of the parts of this checklist.

Suggested Roles — Criteria

This is for the work product lead (i.e., the person calling the inspection). This is meant to provide guidance on what types of people should participate in this inspection and how to apportion inspection focus. On one implementation, the process group created this part of the inspection checklist for all the leads. It also allowed the process group to revisit this for process improvement purposes. Because there is a 1:1 relationship of inspection checklist to work product, you can tailor this for any particular work product.

Entry Criteria

This is for the author. Because inspection checklists are tightly coupled to a particular work product, place all the mind-jogger items that the author needs to address in each and every inspection checklist prior to inspection submittal. For documents, you might see things like:

- "Check header format for correct fields"
- "Make sure TOC updated"
- "Check footer"
- "Has document been spell-checked?"
- "Were new acronyms added and included in acronym list?"

For coding, you might see things like:

- "Has Lint been run?"
- "Has coding header been checked and updated?"

These are all the kinds of things that the author needs to do before an inspection. You can tailor these mind-jogger items based on the individual work product. This is a powerful pre-inspection quality gate by the author that is totally integrated into the inspection checklist.

Inspection Criteria

Subdivide all your inspection checklist items by roles. Consciously think about what kinds of inspectors will participate in this inspection and what questions and statements apply best to them versus questions and statements for other types of inspectors. For example, it makes no sense for technical people to look at portions of a document that are not technical! You can assign a nontechnical person to do that. The point here is that you can significantly improve the quality of the inspection itself by matching roles to inspection topics. Tailor this criteria segregation by the target work product. With this separation, the inspection lead can now assign certain criteria to certain inspectors — not just adopt an "inspect this" mentality. For critical sections, the lead can assign multiple sets of eyes to go over that same section. The lead can also instruct inspector A to apply those checklist items to one section while instructing inspector B to apply those same checklist items to another section. If the lead adheres to the role-criteria guidelines, an inspector can be directed to that part of the inspection checklist for instructions. I am a great believer in including your internal customer as part of the inspection team. What better way is there to address customer concerns directly and, at the same time, improve quality? If your customer is saying things like "if only George had checked for this, I wouldn't have to keep fixing this!" the customer now can directly get that inspection checklist upgraded for this continuing defect.

I want to point out that, in the real world, you will start out with a sparse population of inspection checklists. You will develop these over time, reaching the goal of having an inspection checklist per work product in your end-to-end life cycle. You will start out with inspections where there are no inspection checklists. In that event, work product leads make their best judgments about who become inspectors and what they are to inspect.

Work Product Guidelines

This third member of the work product set is optional. For complex work products, you might need some helpful hints to help that developer or author to create or update that work product. Work product guidelines are particularly helpful when you definitely do *not* want any embedded guidelines in the main template.

Document work products quite often embed the guidelines in the template in the form of hidden text or italicized colored text. For documents, placing those helpful hints right where real information is to go makes a lot of sense. Separate guidelines may be more appropriate for some documents.

It is a great area to place coding guidelines or standards for coding work products. If you have a C++ coding work product, then C++ coding guidelines are appropriate here. Coding work products are such that embedded guidelines are not welcome. I want to diverge a little here and get on another soapbox related to the terms "guidelines" versus "standards." I have heard many who use these terms interchangeably. They are very different process elements. Guidelines are helpful hints and recommended approaches to doing things. *They do not represent absolute requirements that must be followed*. Standards are requirements that *must be followed*. This distinction is important for this process model:

■ Guidelines or standards that are associated with a particular work product go with that work product's set in the support level.
■ Guidelines that go beyond any particular work product are physically placed in one of the work product sets affected while aliases are placed in any other work product affected. This ties all the affected work products to the common guidelines while retaining one copy of the guidelines.

- Standards that go beyond any particular work product are part of the authority level. These requirements will require traceability to process elements and have a traceability matrix like other authority-level elements.

For the reasons stated above, I am a great believer in choosing "guidelines" versus "standards" when talking about coding. In my experience, many coding standards are truly coding guidelines anyway.

Work Product Example(s)

This fourth member of the work product set is optional. I really believe that people learn rapidly from seeing examples. In my implementations, I encouraged leads to provide me with examples that they were proud of. I would place these examples on the process intranet within minutes of receiving them. I noticed some rather interesting people-related aspects related to examples. Leads vied to get their examples included in the process world. Leads made extra efforts to produce quality products for an expanding presence in the process repository. We could add examples or replace better examples with lesser ones. In a nutshell, our examples became better and better very naturally. As more things showed up in the process world that were "owned" by people, the higher probability you had that people would continue building quality products. There was pride of ownership by allowing this. Other leads subconsciously pushed for their examples to also show up. They made extraordinary efforts to produce quality products because their visibility became greater than they could achieve otherwise. I learned a long time ago that my customer's comments and inputs were important whereas mine didn't count. In the process world, my customers are also my practitioner users. This software process model capitalizes on this concept.

Forms

Forms are process elements that are primarily associated with procedures. In this software process model, variations of procedural solutions quite often have associative differences in the supporting forms. You might run into a form usage that is invoked directly from an activity. These are rare — but can happen.

With this process model, you should be able to take any form and identify which procedure or activity created, used, or updated it. I should be able to create a form-centric matrix that provides that story.

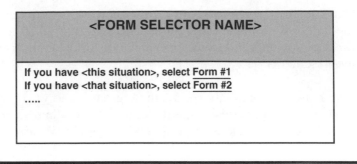

Figure 8.3   Form selector format.

The sheer presence of any form is yet another piece of auditable evidence that something was "done."

Just like work products, I realized a long time ago that when talking about this thing called a "form," you really have:

- Variations of forms consistent with how-to variances.
- An associative set of things that collectively go with each form. I call this group of things the "form set."

To address form variances, this software process model has a similar method to the work product selector called a form selector. This provides the needed flexibility and extensibility at the form level by selecting the appropriate form. A form selector looks like Figure 8.3.

Like work products, you will find this particularly useful when you really want form variances to provide forms in a single class.

The form set is composed of the following:

- The form template
- The form inspection checklist
- The form guidelines
- The form example(s)

The first bullet item should always be there unless your form is a built-in tool-based form. *(Initially, you'll have form template holes until your process repository becomes more robust.)* The last three bullet items are optional.

You get to a form set:

- From a hyperlinked form reference within procedures or activities
- From a Web page reference to a list of form sets — which in turn hyperlink to any particular form set

The form set, like the work product set, is an important concept in this software process model. You will find that changes to a form template invariably change other members of the set. For example, a form template change could affect the optional inspection checklist, optional guidelines, and form examples.

Form Template

This first member of the form set is absolutely essential to the success of your process execution. Like the work product, the form template may be implied if you are using a professional tool. For other cases, you'll need to create a form template. If you're asking someone to fill in a form, you need to supply what the form looks like. That's where the form template comes in.

Form Inspection Checklist

This second member of the form set is only needed when you have complex forms requiring a quality inspection. Simple forms really don't need a form inspection checklist.

Form Guideline

This member of the form set may be needed for complex forms. Typically, most forms do not need a form guideline.

Form Example(s)

This last member of the form set comes into play when it is useful to actually have filled-in forms as examples.

Project Records

The final part of this layer contains the metadata related to project performance. This is also an important aspect of CMMI compliance. The types of records stored here are meant for easy access. You store actual data from your financial systems related to:

- Actuals by executed activities
- Actuals by executed activity groups
- Actuals by executed phase
- Actuals by system parts across all activities based on all executed activities related to those parts, etc.

You can do this easily with this software process model because there is a direct correlation of schedule tasking to process activities to time charging. They are all aligned totally for that real-world connection.

If you are building a program made up of certain software subsystems, wouldn't it be nice to know your previous costs related to similar parts? Notice that I use the term "costs," because accurate pricing is based on accurate cost estimates. Costing and pricing are two different things. It can be disastrous to base a price of $8 million on a declared cost of $10 million (taking a known $2 million loss for new entry into a business area) when the actual cost is $18 million (losing $10 million versus $2 million). Businesses that do this will surely die. You simply can't survive basing price on bad cost estimates. This is why this part of this layer is critical and is built into this software process model method.

Before I go on, I want to make it clear that we are not storing project records here that make up all the delivered and nondelivered artifacts for any and all projects. These types of records belong with the project — usually in a configuration management repository. What we are storing here are project metarecords related to process performance (i.e., to capture the cost of executing activities and the cost of creating a system part, etc.). These rightly belong in the process repository.

Chapter 9

Side 2 — Training

Training Packages

Having discussed the four main layers of side 1 of the pyramid, we now turn our attention to side 2 of the pyramid — the training aspect of this model.

Just like our original assertion that not all "whats" need "how-tos," not all process elements or areas need training packages. I found that training packages were needed:

- For an understanding of this process model
- For an understanding of the end-to-end process story
- For critical process elements (e.g., your inspection procedure)
- For complex process elements
- For role-specific training
- For functional area training (e.g., requirements management, sub-contract management, and business development)
- For external standard requirements compliance (e.g., ISO 9001)
- For regulation compliance
- When the organization felt it was necessary

I may be at odds with many people, but I consider "awareness training" as merely covering the summary or introduction of a regular training package. If you consider a training package as being an overview or summary portion and an elaboration portion, then awareness training just covers the first portion. This separation addresses an internal customer (company) need to have both light training and in-depth training. Training budgets can be tight and this allows flexibility for training.

PowerPoint is a marvelous office tool to address training packages. Once a PowerPoint presentation is produced, you can set it up for a slideshow display, you can hyperlink to it, and you can create instructor notes pages. You can even set up hyperlinks within the presentation to the real process item and allow normal "back" traversal to occur when using it. All in all, this basic MS Office tool can be a powerful partner to an understanding of this process world.

How do we get to all this training? Before answering this question, we need to go back to the basic organization of our software process model organized over four layers in side 1 of the pyramid. Training packages are associated with various process elements, layers, or views. That association has a direct bearing on how you get to these training packages and where they reside on side 2. Here's that breakdown.

General Training

- Process framework architecture training. This training provides the big picture to the entire process framework architecture. This training package is reached from:
    - Top-level process Web page ("general training")
    - Web-based training list
- General metric collection process framework architecture training. This training is aimed at how the entire process framework architecture deals with metrics collection and how it is passed off to metrics folks who convert data into useful information. This training package is reached from:
    - Top-level process Web page ("general training")
    - Web-based training list
- General scheduling process framework architecture training. This training is aimed at a project manager, development manager, or lead to relate how the static process activities relate to project schedule task instances. Topics like work breakdown structures and time charging are also part of this course. This training package is reached from:
    - Top-level process Web page ("general training")
    - Web-based training list

Functional Area Training

■ Functional area training. These areas can be topic-based functional areas or role-based functional areas. Training can cover topics like "requirements management," "new business acquisition," and "configuration management." These kinds of training packages are reached from:

- Web-based training list

Authority-Level Training

■ Company policy awareness training. This training is suitable for new hires or transferred personnel to make everyone aware of the company policies and their associated process elements that deal with those policies. This training package is reached from:
- Authority-level hyperlink from "company policies"
- Web-based training list
■ International standards training. This training is suitable at two levels. Awareness training is suitable for all hands whereas an in-depth training is more suitable for process groups, quality folks, and internal auditors. This training package is reached from:
- Authority-level hyperlink from "ISO 9001 standard," etc.
- Web-based training list
■ Maturity model training. This training is also suitable at two levels. Awareness training is suitable for everyone whereas an in-depth training is more suitable for process groups, quality folks, and internal auditors. This training package is reached from:
- Authority-level hyperlink from "CMM," "SE-CMM," or "CMMI," etc.
- Web-based training list

Repeatable-Level Training

■ Business-area (horizontal end-to-end) process framework architecture training. This training provides the major business-area end-to-end activity story as shown in the top-level Web page. This training package is reached from:
- Top-level process Web page ("general training")
- Web-based training list

■ Life-cycle phase (including "swim lanes") framework architecture training. This training takes a horizontal view of the major life-cycle phases as shown on the top-level Web page and addresses all the interdisciplinary roles and functions for that phase. This training package is reached from:
 – Top-level process Web page ("general training")
 – Web-based training list
■ Activity-based training. This training is specific training required to be successful at executing a particular activity. Typically, these training packages point to commercial offerings in addition to company offerings. This type of training can directly relate to specific roles and thus can be part of anyone's expertise. This training package is reached from:
 – Training portion of the activity requiring that training
 – Web-based training list

Implementation-Level Training

■ Procedure training. Not all procedures need training packages. I would certainly have training for broad-based procedures like the inspection procedure, the corrective action procedure, the focus group procedure, the postmortem procedure, etc. These training packages are reached from:
 – The procedure where training is needed
 – Web-based training list

Support-Level Training

■ Work product training. I would limit work product training to just the complex work products, tool-based work products, or critical work products. Not all work products need training packages. Examples and templates can suffice. These training packages are reached from:
 – Work product set area
 – Work product guidelines
 – Web-based training list
■ Forms training. Very few forms need training packages. A good form should be self-explanatory. If needed, these training packages are reached from:
 – Form set area
 – Form guidelines
 – Web-based training list

Although the various training packages should be organized in one area, it can be desirable to subdivide the training package locations to the general breakdown described above. For our implementations, we always wanted a single Web "button" to get to all the training packages displayed in an alphabetized list — no matter where you were in the process hierarchy.

Not all process elements or process areas require training packages. The best process element of all is totally self-sufficient and is self-evident as to its usage. Training packages are really needed to tie things together for that big-picture perspective and understanding. Classic examples are things like "requirements management." This is an umbrella term for a whole host of schedulable things (activities) and includes procedural how-tos and shows up as part of other activities (like allocation of requirements as part of design decomposition). If you want people to really understand this thing called requirements management, you'll cover all aspects of this term. Another great place where training packages exist is role-based training. Think about it — if we identify roles per activity, then we can identify all the things that we expect that role to do! This kind of training package is absolutely marvelous for new hires, transferred employees, and newly promoted employees who take on new roles.

Chapter 10

Side 3 — Process Traceability

Process Traceability for Compliance

This side of the pyramid is particularly important for your process group and for external auditors and assessors. It is where we place all the various compliance matrices to demonstrate that our processes meet those requirements, goals, and maturity model key practices.

Examples are:

- Company policy compliance matrix
- ISO 9001 standard compliance matrix
- CMMI compliance matrix
- Government standard compliance matrix
- Government regulation compliance matrix

A company should not write company policies unless they have some assurance that these policies are translated into actions. These actions are the process elements such as activities and procedures. The beauty of this software process model is simple: Follow the process and you follow policies.

The Software Productivity Consortium (SPC) produced a comprehensive spreadsheet to focus on the SW-CMM. This spreadsheet allowed users to:

■ Map process compliance to the key practices and goals of the key process areas (KPAs) of the SW-CMM
■ Relate generic work product names to your specific company work product equivalents
■ Relate generic roles to your specific company role equivalents
■ Tailor the SW-CMM to your business

This completed spreadsheet is a great artifact to present to any external SW-CMM assessors to show how your processes address the SW-CMM. You can also produce your own compliance matrix. Adding formulas in columns allows you to fold up compliance percentages to each process area, for each goal, and for all maturity levels automatically as process evidence artifacts are identified against the model statements. Compliance matrices make getting that successful appraisal or assessment a slam dunk.

As of this writing, there are equivalent compliance matrices for the various models of the CMMI (staged and continuous) in the form of spreadsheets, databases, and tool offerings. I prefer a spreadsheet to keep things simple. The spreadsheet has the added advantage that more people know Excel than Access and may not have specific tool knowledge. In addition, you can send an Excel spreadsheet as an attachment to any auditor or assessor and it is readable by a standard MS Office application. The KISS (Keep It Simple, Stupid) principle is great here.

If you are ISO 9001 certified (or want to be), create a spreadsheet with the ISO standards requirements down one side with a single column and mark which process elements work for each and every requirement. Again, this is a powerful artifact to give your external ISO 9001 auditor for standards compliance. A robust spreadsheet will almost certainly translate into success for certification or recertification.

For those companies that have to comply with government regulations, create a compliance matrix for each and every set of regulations. The regulators will love it.

All of these compliance matrices are to be created and maintained by your process group. These allow you to have a single directive to your practitioners "following the process." The average practitioner does not need to know all the authority-level stuff because of these compliance matrices.

I did work at one company that had a real problem with this concept. Supplying compliance matrices to external auditors and assessors was a foreign concept. This company came from the position that you don't give anything out voluntarily! That same company had an awful time getting a successful CMM assessment rating. These compliance matrices are just that important.

IMPLEMENTING THE SOFTWARE PROCESS MODEL

II

Chapter 11

Side 4 — Process Repository Implementation

Web-Based Version-Control Process Repository

Before getting into the Web implementation, a key part of this software process method is the makeup of the process repository itself.

Separate Master Control from Web Presentation

You can place all the process elements in a conventional Configuration Management Library (CML) for the standard master repository. This master repository can be version controlled manually via folder names or via a version-controlled tool for automatic version control. If you're interested only in master storage, almost any CML tool will do for master process repository storage. Tools like ClearCase will do just fine for a straight master repository where:

- Master storage is the focus, not direct Web access.
- You're not interested in direct application accessibility on stored CML files.

This CML approach ends up with two process repositories:

■ Master storage
■ Active Web storage

You need to manage the master process repository and make sure that updates show up in the active Web area on those updates. One place I worked chose this approach and had the quality organization (ugh) manage this. This particular place had territorial wars over control of this area. Should control reside with:

■ The quality organization?
■ The configuration management organization?
■ The process group?

The correct answer, in my opinion, is the last one. The same group that creates the process elements and controls all changes to that base should manage the process repository. The CM group can fit here if, and only if, it is a service function to the process group.

The downsides of this process repository duality are:

■ You have two areas that will always need to be synchronized.
■ You can introduce errors by updating the master and failing to update the current Web version. This could be a monumental maintenance problem unless discipline is used.
■ There is a built-in delay to process updates as seen on the Web. That is, a crucial update has been made on the master but the Web does not reflect the change yet.
■ You can't directly update the artifact actually presented on the Web. You have to update the master and then update the Web version.

Integrated Master Control with Web Presentation

A far better approach is to integrate the master repository with your Web presentation. Have one and only one repository that:

■ Provides a process structure for process elements
■ Provides Web access capability
■ Provides versioning control
■ Provides access rights and privileges
■ Provides an alias capability

I have personally used two tools that fit the bill very nicely for this process repository:

- LiveLink
- SharePoint

Both are Web-based versioning control tools that allowed various accessibility rights. LiveLink was a whole lot easier to set up structures with than SharePoint. LiveLink allowed aliases to files whereas SharePoint appeared not to be able to do that (as of this writing). This alias capability allowed one physical file with pointers to that file in other areas of the structure. This is a fundamental database concept to have one and only one file structure — not replications elsewhere. I was not able to get SharePoint to do this. SharePoint did allow me to set up my top-level Web page on their home page so that a SharePoint user would see the same view as a direct Web user (not via SharePoint).

The beauty of both of these product offerings is that any update automatically goes live on your intranet. Think about it:

- You can maintain all your versions in the repository. This is critical for any process repository because different projects may have different process bases on which they're operating. Maintaining different versions is absolutely critical in the process world. In the software process model method, versions are identified by a single date — hopefully via a tag in the markup language embedded in your files. For those of you that came from a paper document environment, get rid of the notion that you have to have revision letters, etc. You just need a single date. There are some good reasons for this:
  - If you format your dates as YYYY/MM/DD, you can really simplify date searches. This is a natural sort order rather than the American way of having the MM/DD/YYYY format. If your date-based software is smart, go ahead and use the American form — otherwise, go with the YYYY/MM/DD format. Make it easy on yourself.
  - You can create a script to search on date tags that automatically identify the process basis for any project. Every project has a start date. You use this single piece of information to identify the latest date to this start date without exceeding it to get the process basis for any project.
  - You want to change process elements at will. Standard revision letters get absurd in the process world. Do you really want your revisions to start at "A" and go to "Z," then "AA" through

"ZZ," etc.? I don't think so. I've been in businesses that have restricted changes solely because of revision numbers cycling too much for documents. This is a case of the tail wagging the dog. We don't want these restrictions for process elements. We want to make process changes rapidly.

■ Non-tip (or the latest version) is in the repository — not displayed on the Web. You need to be able to get to older versions, but don't make it so easy. Dates will identify any older version quite nicely. There will be a natural incentive to step up to the latest version as the latest version is the one on your intranet Web site. I have always advocated that projects should not automatically chase the tail of process improvement. Trying to keep current on an ever-changing process basis just creates chaos.

■ The latest version or "tip" is the version presented on your intranet Web for instant Web access. This allows standard "check-out" and "check-in" operations to get Web updates done. You can always know the official Web version. It's the "tip" version of any file within the process repository. Look at how simple the change control becomes for process changes by the process group:
  - Identify the process element for change.
  - Check out the process element to be changed.
  - If it is a cosmetic change, make the change and conduct a simplified review of the change. If it is a substantial change, make the change and conduct an inspection of the changes.
  - Change the displayed date.
  - Make the "saved-as" HTML version if you are operating at the standard MS Office suite level. You won't need to do this if directly changing the HTML version.
  - Check in the updated process element (or elements). This automatically updates both the repository and the Web.

■ You can use standard MS Office work products to produce your HTML files. This allows almost anyone in your organization to maintain your process repository. No special Web master is needed. The latest MS Office products have built-in "save as HTML" or "save as a single Web page" features. What this means is that you can create all your process elements using your favorite application. This could be ideal for small companies. You don't need a Web guru to implement this software process method at all.

■ You can readily embed hyperlinks throughout your process elements to other process elements — using standard MS Office products. I used Word, Excel, and PowerPoint extensively for process elements. You can embed hyperlinks in these standard files and the links get activated once files are saved as Web pages.

In SharePoint, I saved both the ".doc" files and their ".htm" equivalents. This allowed me to change the standard file in Word, Excel, PowerPoint, etc., update the standard file and then "save as a single Web page" for the Web-based file. For user visibility, I kept the file name prefix the same and added ".doc" for the standard file and ".web" for the Web equivalent. This provided yet another visual marker to distinguish them. Do what makes sense to you.

■ The latest version of anything is automatically what is "on the Web." There's no misunderstanding at all about this.

Chapter 12

Side 4 — Intranet Web Implementation

Intranet Basics

Before I get into this topic in earnest, I want to make a big point about the process world. There are two aspects of processes that are equally important:

- Content integrity
- Presentation/access integrity

This reminds me of constant bickering while I was in the military about whether the air crew is more or less important than the ground crew. The answer is that both are equally important. You simply can't have one without the other.

I mention this because (believe it or not) there are people out there who seem to think that if you write a process-related sentence somewhere in a document or place a bulleted line item in a training package, you somehow have that process topic covered. Workers at one company actually felt that if they merely added these process statements to a pile of other process stuff they were finished. Somehow, process practitioners would hopefully find these magic statements and all would be well with the world. At one workplace, my boss did not understand this critical aspect for success. I was ordered to remove this aspect when trying to run a process group. The order was to just write process stuff and forget all the other garbage. I had to become very creative to work around this ignorance. It was extremely difficult to get anything developed in the process world that would end up in the success column because of this management stance. People who know me know that I'm passionate about process and I'm not willing to purposely create process disasters.

This book primarily addresses the presentation/access part of this via this process framework architecture. You can have absolutely wonderful process content but if people can't find that content or can't be bothered to scroll down voluminous documents, etc., to find anything, it doesn't matter what you have. Conversely, if you provide easy access to process elements but they are considered poor for content, you don't have anything. Remember, both are important and need equal attention from your process group.

I have to remind process-group members that we should not treat process as a holy relic. The antiquity professionals go over lots and lots of ancient texts to find that gem of wisdom buried somewhere in that input. Process users do not want to go through tons and tons of "chaff" words to find those important "kernel" gems of wisdom. They want the opposite. They want to get to what they want in as few clicks as possible and have the whole thing on one Web page with minimal to no scrolling. Over the years, I have observed that this is probably the biggest reason why the best of process solutions fail. They do not address ease of use and don't connect processes to the real world — hence, this book.

A poorly written résumé will get discarded if it doesn't grab someone's attention within 20 seconds. The same phenomenon occurs in the process world. Go right to what people want and provide a rapid access to the process "meat." Off-load the process chaff for those who really want to take a trip through memory lane for extra elaborations. If you don't do this, process practitioners will simply discard or not use your process. Keep in mind that process is there to support the organization, not the other way around! I've run into process people who have lost sight of this important concept. In those environments, process has taken on a life of its own with a full bureaucracy to support process. I am a firm believer that "small is beautiful" for process — don't get carried away with writing process for the sheer sake of writing process.

The Web format provides an incredible opportunity to rapidly get to things and off-load verbose things via hyperlinks. With simple Web-page access counts, you can even do fairly sophisticated process improvement based on real data. If you exist in a document-centric company, you'll have huge difficulties with a Web solution, because such a culture insists on document headers on the Web — which wastes valuable screen display space. People used to documents cannot make the distinction between paper documents and Web representations. I know because I have been in these environments. If you question this way of thinking, you'll get attacked.

Side 4 provides the total enchilada view of the selective processes in this software process model. A Web-based, version-controlled process environment really "makes it" for implementation.

On one implementation, we were able to use a product called LiveLink for our process elements repository. LiveLink is a Web-based versioning control tool that allows:

- Direct URL hyperlinking into LiveLink to access the latest version of anything. This is a powerful capability to be able to pick up the latest process element instantly on "check in."
- Simple "check in/check out" for process element updates. This allows a simple process-group capability to "check out" process elements, update them, and, on "check in," have that same element go "live" on the process intranet.
- Versioned Word and PowerPoint objects. This allows all the activities, procedures, work products, forms, training, and compliance matrices to be versioned and directly accessible on the intranet. The Word files can be standard Word files or HTML files (because Word can "save as HTML").
- Direct access to LiveLink directories and subdirectories. This allows direct hyperlink capability to the internal LiveLink structures. This became particularly useful for Web-based lists because the list contents always reflected reality and the lists were always in alphabetical order naturally.

There are some important aspects of the intranet presentation that need to be in place:

- Make sure that all process Web pages have an HTML-tagged date field. I've had a huge problem with various companies about this aspect of process element identification. In the process world, you want things to change for process improvement purposes. I've worked for companies that have insisted on revisions, headers, and dates on process elements as if they were documents. Can you imagine the problems of going from Rev A...Z, AA...ZZ, AAA...ZZZ, etc., for process elements? If you use a single date field as the "version," you can readily identify the entire process basis for any project by merely supplying a start date for that project. Any process element closest to (but not later than) that date is that project's process basis. Even a script can do this. HTML is a tagged language that can readily do this.

■ Make sure that all process Web pages have a common set of traversal buttons to get to various process areas. One implementation had that common set along the side and another implementation had it across the top of each Web page. My personal preference was across the X-axis — either the top or bottom but not along the side. That set of traversal buttons needs to be absolutely consistent across the Web displays. These traversal areas point to ordered lists:

1. Process "Home" — Top-level root node for life-cycle Process Activity Diagrams (PADs) and Event Driver Procedures (EDP) lists. You always need a way to get to the absolute top of the process area.

2. Phases list. This is a list of the same Phases found in that top-level Web page. Always provide multiple ways of getting at things. Ideally, the hyperlink will take you inside the versioning control tool to the Phases folder where all PADs and EDP lists reside.

3. Inputs/stimuli list. This provides yet another way to find the correct process element if you just select the correct input or stimulus. Ideally, the hyperlink will take you inside the versioning control tool to the inputs/stimuli folder where all inputs/stimuli are listed. Each input/stimulus can be further set up to hyperlink to the correct process element that acts on that item.

4. Outputs/responses list. Like the inputs/stimuli list, this provides yet another way to find the correct process element if you just know the output side of that process element. Ideally, the hyperlink will take you inside the versioning control tool to the outputs/responses folder where all outputs/responses are listed. Each output/response can be further set up to hyperlink to the correct process element that produced that item.

5. Activity list. An alphabetized list of all the activities in the software process repository. Ideally, the hyperlink will take you inside the versioning control tool to the activities folder where all activities reside.

6. Roles list. Ideally, the hyperlink will take you inside the versioning control tool to the roles folder where all roles involved with process are listed. On one implementation, this roles list was really an Excel spreadsheet that showed "roles" down one side and "process elements" across the other. This shows where certain roles show up and can be invaluable for role-based training.

7. How selectors list. An alphabetized list of how selectors in the software process repository. Ideally, the hyperlink will take you inside the versioning control tool to the how selectors folder where all how selectors reside.

8. Procedures list. An alphabetized list of all the procedures in the software process repository. Ideally, the hyperlink will take you inside the versioning control tool to the procedures folder where all procedures reside. Work instructors can also be placed here.

9. Work product selectors list. An alphabetized list of all the work product selectors in the software process repository. Ideally, the hyperlink will take you inside the versioning control tool to the work product selectors folder where all work product selectors reside.

10. Work product sets list. An alphabetized list of work product sets in the software process repository. Ideally, the hyperlink will take you inside the versioning control tool to the work product sets folder where all work product sets reside. A work product set includes up to four kinds of things: the work product template, the work product inspection checklist, the work product guideline, and the work product example(s).

11. Form selectors list. An alphabetized list of all form selectors in the software process repository. Ideally, the hyperlink will take you inside the versioning control tool to the form selectors folder where all form selectors reside.

12. Form sets list. An alphabetized list of form sets in the software process repository. Ideally, the hyperlink will take you inside the versioning control tool to the form sets folder where all form sets reside. A form set includes up to four kinds of things: the form template, the form inspection checklist, the form guideline, and the form example(s).

13. Training packages list. An alphabetized list of all the training packages in the software process repository. Ideally, the hyperlink will take you inside the versioning control tool to the training packages folder where all training packages reside. (I found it more useful to place all the training packages in a single folder rather than segregate them by process level scope.)

14. Compliance matrices list. An alphabetized list of all compliance matrices in the software process repository. Ideally, the hyperlink will take you inside the versioning control tool to the compliance matrices folder where all compliance matrices reside.

15. Authorities list. An alphabetized list of all the authorities (at the authority level) in the software process repository. Ideally, the hyperlink will take you inside the versioning control tool to the authorities folder where all subfolders reside for things like ISO 9001, CMMI, company policies, etc.

For the LiveLink implementation, we were able to point directly to the appropriate LiveLink structure to pick all this up knowing that it is totally correct all the time.

I determined a long time ago that users get very upset if they can't escape out of where they are in a convenient fashion. Having to press "back," "back," "back"... is not a good Web traversal practice.

- Make sure that most process Web pages can be seen on a single monitor display screen. The following should all be single Web pages without scroll bars (or minimal scroll bars):
    - Top-level Web page
    - PADs and EDPs
    - Activities
    - How selectors
    - Work product selectors
    - Form selectors

The other process elements may need scroll bars. These often need to be printed out:
    - Any list
    - Procedures and work instructions
    - Work product templates
    - Work product checklists
    - Work product guidelines
    - Work product example(s)
    - Form templates
    - Form checklists
    - Form guidelines
    - Form example(s)
    - Full training packages
    - Compliance matrices
- Color code process elements for a direct and quick confirmation of those process elements that have standard forms. These include:
    - Activities. I used yellow to agree with the general-purpose project management PROPS life-cycle model. You may use any color. You may also color code "swim lane" activity differences.

- How selectors. Select a color.
- Work product selector. Select a color.
- Form selector. Select a color.

Once selected, color gives a powerful visual confirmation to the process Web user that they have what they want. Over time, the color will become institutionalized in people's thinking about processes.

Now that I have described the basics of a Web implementation, you should have a good feel for what common traversals are needed on all process Web pages.

Major Functional Breakdown for Process — Don't Do This

Before organizing your repeatable level of activities or PADs, I need to steer you away from organizing all your processes into major company functions. It's a huge mistake.

I had one experience where leads at a company took a look at their business and determined that the top-level Web process breakdown should be topics like:

- Manage the enterprise
- Support the enterprise
- Manage the product
- Build the product
- Support the product
- Manufacture the product

At first glance, you could look at this list and tell yourself that you could take all parts of your business and probably find a home for one of these categories. A closer look at this list reveals that only two items ("Build the product" and "Manufacture the product") have life cycles; the remainders are essentially asynchronously driven based on those life cycles! In other words, you mix apples and oranges right off the bat. I will now describe why this process division is bad and how you can achieve the same end result with a life-cycle process approach using this software process model.

Even though this company had a what/how separation, they actually created stovepipes of process. The term "stovepipe" is used to signify that process elements are "owned" by an organizational element in a vertical fashion — as if they were jammed into a stovepipe. This division created:

■ Wholly owned activities by one company entity (e.g., this is an engineering activity, that one is a manufacturing activity, etc.). The big problem here is that, in the real world, other roles may be affected when executing process activities.

■ Wholly owned activities can have outputs that go to another wholly owned activity in another part of the company. This company ended up with transfer of data flows that went into the ether because the two process elements were not engaged. There were process disconnects all over the place. The problems here are obvious — you cannot have disconnected processes and win.

■ From an enterprise perspective, it might be clear that process changes need to be made in one area, but workarounds are introduced because of the immovable position of the first area's process owner. Again, you end up with no enterprise-level arbiter to make sure that process changes occur where they should occur.

■ This mapping creates a set of "process owners" — one per process breakdown. You see things like the engineering VP in charge of "Build the product," for example. You have now created a committee with none of them wearing the enterprise hat. They will all be protecting their own power and territory! The problem here is that you have fragmented ownership of your processes. No one is in charge.

My message is clear: Don't do this. Don't have organizational process owners, but do have a process group that has an enterprise perspective on process.

I have walked into an environment like this. The processes were useless and not followed but the various process owners defended their turf to the death. When I basically told this company "the emperor has no clothes on" for process, I immediately became a target for removal. I became a threat to those who invested their time and money in this awful way to subdivide process ownership.

What the company really wanted was to identify where certain roles (associated with organizational elements) fit. The software process model is role-based in a real-world integrated team sense. Using my model, you can readily determine where certain roles fit in, no matter who the predominant "owner" of the activity or procedure is.

You need to map your process world onto one or more life cycles. That is the only way you really connect your processes to the real world and make that process/tasking connection. Let's proceed to what you need to do.

Multi-Life Cycles for Process

Some companies have more than one life cycle in which processes are involved. Examples might be a development life cycle and a service life cycle. In this software process model approach, we recognize this fact by segregating each life-cycle root node Web page as separate and distinct process mappings. When this happens, I suggest you provide hyperlinks from your company intranet home page to the appropriate process root Web page. To make absolutely sure that your process users get to the correct Web page, identify projects or organizational entities as one or the other.

The software process model approach really starts at these process root node Web pages but does recognize that you might have more than one life-cycle model for processes. For that reason, this multi–life cycle top-level connection is outside the bounds of this book.

Top-Level Root Web Page

A top-level root Web page exists for each life-cycle model in which you wish to map processes. This Web page provides an entire end-to-end process story for any given life cycle.

This process approach subdivides any life cycle into two main horizontal slices:

- Schedulable process world
- Nonschedulable process world.

We break down the former into PADs. We break down the latter into event-driven procedures, or EDPs. On drill-downs, when you see any PAD, you also see an EDP because both exist at any given point in time along the life-cycle time-line.

From a vertical perspective, the software process model approach divides the entire end-to-end life cycle first into segments and then into phases. As you will see, a segment is composed of one or more phases. The phase is the lowest software process entity to represent any PAD.

Given this general description, the top-level page should look something like Figure 12.1.

From this life-cycle process home page (and all other process Web pages), you can traverse to any of the selections on the top traversal bar. The traversal bar is common to all process Web pages in this software process method.

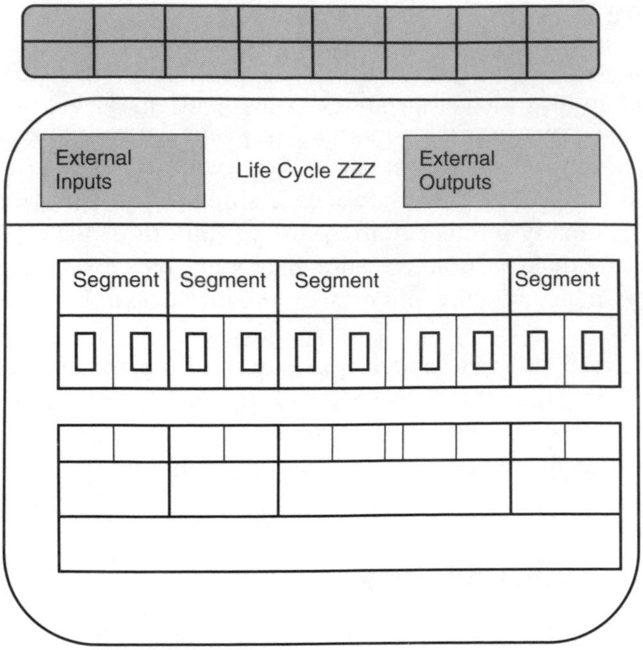

Figure 12.1 Top-level Web page.

All the input and output hyperlinks in the traversal bar should ideally link right to the version-controlled process repository in the appropriate folder where these list files reside. Once there, the standard Web-based "back" button will return you to your original Web page.

After the common top portion, the life-cycle root Web page is divided into three main horizontal sections:

- The life-cycle identification section — along with the major inputs/outputs for this life cycle
- The schedulable processes for this life cycle
- The nonschedulable processes for this life cycle

Identification Portion

When Web users traverse Web pages, it is real important to identify where they are. The intent of this portion of the top-level process Web page is to do just that — identify which life cycle we're talking about. For those enterprises that map out more than one life cycle, it becomes even more important to identify which life cycle we're traversing.

In addition to naming the life cycle, this portion can also provide some very important input/output information at a very high level. As a process person, you really need to know what triggers this life cycle to be implemented. You also need to be clear on what happens after execution — at a very high level. Again, as a process person, you have established anchors from which you can flow down all work products produced as you traverse this life cycle. It provides the basis for complete data-based traceability.

You will notice later that as we drill down from this root-level process Web page, we have almost identical identification portions at the segment and phase Web pages. The differences at the lower levels are:

■ Addition of the segment/phase name to the life-cycle name
■ Specific inputs/stimuli to that segment/phase (versus the entire life cycle)
■ Specific outputs/responses from that segment/phase (versus the entire life cycle)

Schedulable Portion

At the root Web-page level, this schedulable portion shows an entire end-to-end graphical picture subdivided into segments and then finally into phases. This is the one-stop shopping page showing the whole enchilada for this life cycle.

I would advocate actually stating "schedulable processes" on the side of this portion as a visual reinforcement of what we're talking about. At the risk of repeating myself, notice I used "schedulable" versus "scheduled." It has been my experience that early life-cycle tasks may or may not show up on a real schedule. This is particularly true for the DoD contracting companies where the real project schedule only showed up after contract award. Prior to contract award, you may or may not see a precontract schedule — even though schedulable tasks really do exist.

If you do this correctly, you will be very robust on this Web page related to hyperlinks to the drill-down Web pages. If you want to get to a specific segment, you hyperlink on that segment name. If you want to get to a specific phase, you hyperlink on that phase name. On Figure 12.1, I did not show segment and phase names. In reality, this 40,000-foot view may allow you to directly embed segment names but not embed phase names. Embedding phase names might cause the text to be so small that you create an eye chart. Process users will get real upset if they strain their eyes, so don't do this. Web designers can be very creative here by merely numbering phases to provide something from which to hyperlink. You can set up "pass-over" pop-ups to see the real phase names. Keep your users in mind. Remember, "process" is a four-letter word to many people. Anything you can do to make the process experience pleasant and useful for practitioners will be appreciated.

Nonschedulable Portion

At the root Web-page level, this nonschedulable portion shows the same segment/phase mapping as the schedulable portion does. It's like you took the schedulable picture, folded it over, and placed it in the non-schedulable portion for two of the three layers. Like the schedulable portion, this is the one-stop shopping page showing the whole enchilada for event-driven or asynchronous process elements for this life cycle. The three layers shown here represent:

■ Phase-based EDP lists where phases are exact replicas of the schedulable phases
■ Segment-based EDP lists where segments are exact replicas of the schedulable segments
■ Phase/segment-independent EDP lists

Like the presentation issues for the schedulable portion, the same problems exist here. I found that you could directly name (and thus hyperlink) the global lists and segment lists — but not the phase-based lists. Adopt the same solution here as for the schedulable portion: number the phases for hyperlinks and allow pass-over pop-ups for list names.

Like the schedulable portion, I would advocate stating "nonschedulable processes" on the side of this portion as a visual difference from the schedulable portion.

Segment Top-Level Web Page

If you select a segment name from the top-level root page, you get to this segment Web page. This is the Web page that provides one-stop shopping for any and all processes involved with any particular segment. I will remind you that a segment is that portion of any life cycle that is an umbrella term for one or more phases. Examples of segments include "pre-contract" and "contract execution" segments. Both of these segments contain several phases.

From a usability perspective, this second-level Web page will probably not be used much by the average process practitioner. It provides a logical drill-down from the root page that provides that segment view of the process world. I found that different types of managers had a real interest in this view as follows:

- Proposal managers have a real interest in the "pre-contract" segment. That's where a proposal manager's scope lies.
- Project managers have a real interest in the "contract execution" segment. That's where a project manager's scope lies.

Both can see the big picture as to what tasks need to be considered to complete these segments from a scheduling perspective. This view also shows what event-driven procedures can be invoked during this segment. You get to see both the synchronous and asynchronous process world with this view.

Figure 12.2 shows what a segment Web page would look like.

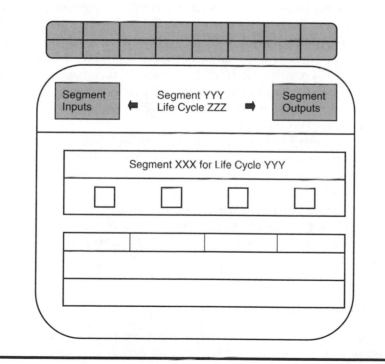

Figure 12.2 Segment top-level Web page.

Just like the root Web page, you can traverse to any of the selections on the top traversal bar. Like the root Web page, the segment Web page is divided into three main horizontal sections:

■ The segment identification section — along with the major inputs/outputs for this segment
■ The schedulable processes for this segment
■ The nonschedulable processes for this segment

Identification Portion

The intent of this portion of the second-level process Web page is to identify which segment we're talking about. For those enterprises that map out more than one life cycle, it becomes even more important to identify which segment of which life cycle we're traversing.

In addition to naming the segment, this portion can also provide some very important input/output information at the segment level. Just as before, you really need to know what triggers this segment to be implemented. You also need to be clear on what happens after segment execution. Like the top-level Web page, you have established anchors from which you can flow down all work products produced as you traverse this life cycle. It provides the basis for complete data-based traceability.

One other piece of information is added here — the left/right traversal arrows. This allows rapid traversal to the previous segment and subsequent segment to ease Web traversal.

As we drill down from this segment process Web page, we have almost identical identification portions at the phase Web pages. The differences at the phase level are:

■ Addition of the phase name to the segment name
■ Specific inputs/stimuli to that phase (versus the entire segment)
■ Specific outputs/responses from that phase (versus the entire segment)

Schedulable Portion

At the segment Web page level, this schedulable portion shows an entire end-to-end segment-based graphical picture subdivided into phases.

You would link on one of these phase PADs if you wanted to see:

■ The specific (external) PAD's inputs/outputs.
■ The specific PAD's end-to-end activities for that part of the life cycle.

- A repeat of the global event-driven processes (for ease of usage
- A repeat of the phase-based event-driven processes (for ease of usage)
- The specific event-driven stimuli, procedures, and responses for that PAD's scope. These event-driven procedures along with their corresponding stimuli/responses are specific for this phase for that life cycle.

Just as before, I would advocate actually stating "schedulable processes" on the side of this portion as a visual reinforcement of what we're talking about.

If you do this segment Web page correctly, you will have robust hyperlinks to the drill-down phase-based Web pages. If you want to get to a specific phase, you hyperlink on that phase name.

Nonschedulable Portion

At the segment Web-page level, this nonschedulable portion shows the same phase mapping as the schedulable portion. Like before, it's like you took the schedulable picture, folded it over, and placed it in the non-schedulable portion for two of the three layers. Like the schedulable portion, this is the one-stop shopping page showing the whole process picture of event-driven or asynchronous process elements for this segment. The three layers shown here represent:

- Phase-based EDP lists where phases are exact replicas of the schedulable phases
- Segment-based EDP lists where segments are exact replicas of the schedulable segments
- Phase/segment-independent EDP lists

Adopt the same solution here as for the schedulable portion: number the phases for hyperlinks and allow pass-over pop-ups for list names.

Like the schedulable portion, I would advocate actually stating "non-schedulable processes" on the side of this portion as a visual difference from the schedulable portion.

Phase Top-Level Web Page

If you select a phase name from either the top-level root page or segment Web page, you get to this phase Web page. This is the Web page that

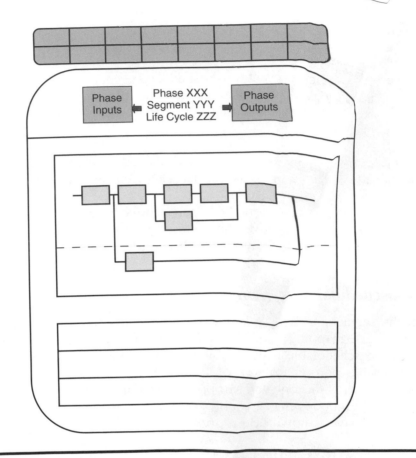

Figure 12.3   Phase top-level Web page.

provides the synchronous and asynchronous process information involved with any particular phase. I will remind you that a phase shows:

- The PAD of synchronous schedulable tasks
- The EDP lists of asynchronous procedures

Figure 12.3 shows what a phase Web page would look like.

Just as before, you can traverse to any of the selections on the top traversal bar. Like all the top-level Web pages, the phase Web page is divided into three main horizontal sections:

- The phase identification section — along with the major inputs and outputs for this phase
- The schedulable processes for this phase — the PAD
- The nonschedulable processes for this phase — the EDP list

Identification Portion

The intent is to identify which phase we're talking about. For those enterprises that map out more than one life cycle, it becomes even more important to identify which phase of which segment of which life cycle we're traversing.

In addition to naming the phases, this portion can also provide some very important inputs and outputs information at the phase level. For this Web page at the phase level, we not only identify inputs and outputs for the synchronous tasks but also identify the stimuli/responses for the asynchronous procedures. That's the big difference between this Web page and the life-cycle Web page or segment Web page. In the real world, people may be aware of what is causing a process action (stimulus) but don't know the name of the procedure, etc. Conversely, they may know the procedure name only and not know the input stimulus. Finally, they may know what the output response is and that's all. I provide multiple ways to get to the procedural element needed for this event-driven procedure to aid process usage by adding stimuli/responses to this phase-based Web page.

One other piece of information is added here — the left/right traversal arrows. This allows rapid traversal to the previous phase and subsequent phase to ease Web traversal.

Just as before, you really need to know what triggers process elements in this phase to be implemented. You also need to be clear about what happens after phase execution. As mentioned, you have established anchors from which you can flow down all work products produced as you traverse this phase, and this provides the basis for complete data-based traceability.

As we drill down from this phase process Web page, we leave the top-level summary Web pages and get to the process "meat." The "meat" may be the process activities (schedulable tasks) or the event-driven procedures (nonschedulable tasks).

Schedulable Portion

At the phase Web-page level, this schedulable portion shows an entire end-to-end phase-based graphical picture showing the predecessor/successor relationships of the process activities involved in this phase. This graphical picture is the PAD.

There will be one PAD per life-cycle phase. In Figure 12.3, activities within the PAD are shown in the center box. The PAD is further subdivided into "swim lanes" to separate engineering from support activities.

I would advocate stating "schedulable processes" on the side of this portion as a visual reinforcement of what we're talking about.

If you do this phase Web page correctly, you will have robust hyperlinks to the drill-down activities and EDP lists.

Nonschedulable Portion

At the phase Web-page level, this nonschedulable portion shows just three layers of EDP lists. The three layers represent:

- Phase-based EDP lists for this phase
- Segment-based EDP lists for the segment in which this phase belongs
- Phase/segment-independent EDP lists

You may notice that I did not include a business-functional area (or horizontal) set of event-driven processes. You can certainly add this if you feel it's necessary. I purposely did not include this horizontal view of event-driven tasks because I want to encourage processes that are not "stovepiped" by business area.

Like for the schedulable portion, I would state "nonschedulable processes" on the side of this portion to create a visual difference from the schedulable portion.

Activity Web Page

The activity Web page is the heart and soul of this process framework model. This is the process element that deals with high-level tasks and can be scheduled. Notice I use the words "can be" because a schedulable task may or may not exist on a real schedule. In this model, I emphasize that we want activity instances on a schedule, however. This is one place where we connect the process world to the real world. We really want that schedule to be the real-world tasking representation or roadmap for work progress.

You want to end up where all schedule tasks have their process counterpart as represented by the process activity. If you had an "Implement Unit" activity in the process world, you may end up with 100 instances of this process element on a project schedule if you had 100 units to be implemented (coded). On a schedule, we use the same reusable (and single) process element targeted to different units and led by different people possibly.

This activity Web page is where you would go if you were "working" that schedule task instance on a project schedule. This one-stop shopping provides you with everything you want to successfully execute that task. The intent is to provide robust hyperlinks to how you do things, from the high-level activity steps, to information about what work products you want produced, and to other useful links.

Stop here and think about how powerful this is. You get total repeatability and a one-click access to all (or most) of the ancillary things that drive most developers crazy without this capability. Having been there, I can attest to the fact that practitioners love this. They can concentrate on what they were hired for — namely computer science, etc. Can you imagine the time saved by showing work product templates and examples right there — rather than hunting for this stuff and possibly getting the wrong one?

The activity page should look something like Figure 12.4. From this page (and all other process Web pages), you can traverse to any of the selections on the top traversal bar.

The activity Web page is the lowest "leaf" of the repeatable level. This page identifies all the predecessor/successor activity relationships relevant to this particular activity. These are shown as hyperlinks to provide that important end-to-end traversal.

The main activity is shown in a tabular form with the activity name shown at the top, with a list of standard identifiers in column 1, and with information specific to this activity in column 2. You can certainly get fancy here and have a graphical representation. I purposely chose this form because:

- It's easy
- You can create a standard table via Word
- More people can maintain your software model–based processes

The real value of this Web page is to provide one-stop shopping related to this activity. We want to embed a lot of hyperlinks here to make this implementation very useful. Here's what I mean:

- Provide a "more" hyperlink after a one-line description.
- Provide hyperlinks from each verb in each step (that has a how-to elaboration) to get you to all the how-to options that you need.
- Provide hyperlinks from work product references to get you to things like templates, inspection checklists, guidelines, and examples. As a process guy, I encouraged better and better examples for the process world. The suppliers of these examples had pride

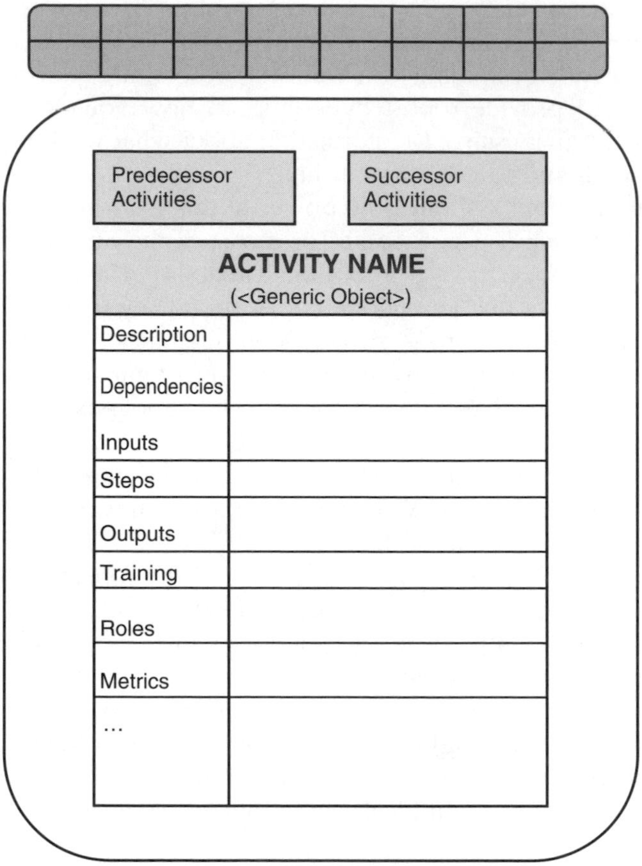

Figure 12.4   Activity Web page.

of ownership and really paid attention to quality to get this visibility privilege.

■ Provide hyperlinks on roles to get to any role description.
■ Provide hyperlinks on metrics to get to metric collection how-to selectors if needed.
■ Provide hyperlinks on training packages needed for activity execution.

How Selector Web Page

The how selector Web page is the way in which we achieve flexibility and extensibility in the how-to procedural world. This software process

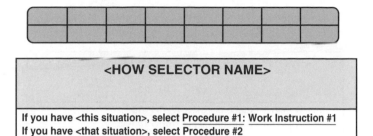

Figure 12.5   How selector Web page.

model encourages "better mousetraps" via this selection capability — a cornerstone of this process approach. I set this model up to always get to a specific procedure through a how selector. I realize there is this one level of indirection — but for process traversal and execution, it is quite acceptable. It is via this mechanism that we get to determine the rationale for selecting this how-to procedure versus that how-to procedure, etc. For those instances where the enterprise wants one and only one procedure selection, we can make that clear, too! I found that this is an incredible mechanism for dealing with multisite differences, scaling differences, etc.

Figure 12.5 shows what a how selector Web page looks like.

You may not realize this but there are more arguments at the how-to level than anywhere else. I've actually seen fistfights over this in the halls of companies. You get into "we do it this way" or "we don't want to do what you do" or "we have a better way" kinds of dialogues. The software process model approach recognizes that there is rarely one and only one way of doing things. This process approach recognizes that the real world needs to deal with different sites, different scaled projects, and different tool sets. This how selector provides all the flexibility you need to select the how-tos appropriate for these differences. The software process model method wants you to have a common, portable "what" level across your projects and divisions while enabling different how-to procedures to allow for site/scope/tool differences.

Work Product Selector Web Page

The work product selector Web page is the way in which we achieve flexibility and extensibility in the work product world. This software

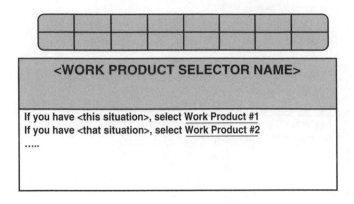

Figure 12.6   Work product selector Web page.

process model recognizes that, like with procedural differences, there may be variances at the work product level. This is yet another key concept within this software process model approach that allows selectability of those work product variances.

Figure 12.6 shows what a work product selector Web page looks like.

You will find this particularly useful when you want work product variances to provide work products in a single class.

Form Selector Web Page

The form selector Web page is the way in which we achieve flexibility and extensibility in the form world. This software process model recognizes that, like with work product differences, there may be variances at the form level. This is yet another key concept within this software process model approach that allows selectability of those form variances.

Figure 12.7 shows what a form selector Web page looks like.

Like work products, you will find this particularly useful when you want form variances to provide forms in a single class.

Procedures

I need to make sure you are aware that the software process method defines the look and feel at the activity or "what" level. The software process method does not define what a procedure looks like. This was done on purpose as follows:

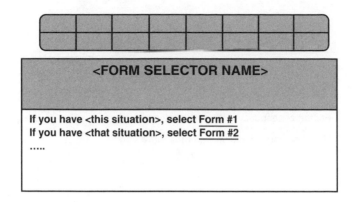

Figure 12.7   Form selector Web page.

- Procedures can range from high-level procedures to low-level procedures.
- The method of getting across any how-to can come in a variety of ways: a flowchart, a checklist, straight verbiage, or a combination of all of these.

In my opinion, a simple mind-jogger checklist describes the most effective procedure. The technical people, with whom I've interfaced, hate piles and piles of words. Keep it simple if possible. If the flowchart effectively represents that how-to, so be it. If a checklist will suffice, so be it.

Having said all that, it is desirable to identify these "leaf" process elements in some consistent fashion — even though the contents vary. I recommend a standard (ideally color coded) header format that clearly identifies this process element as a procedure. Like other process elements in the software process method, I would advocate a date only to identify a procedure version. Get away from using revisions, because it does nothing to connect a process element to a project's process basis. A common procedure header on a Web page could look like Figure 12.8.

Like all other process elements, you just need an identifying name (reinforced with a particular color) and a date.

For those instances where a corresponding low-level work instruction exists, it would be helpful to indicate this and to hyperlink to that corresponding process element. The software process model approach recognizes that we have experienced process users and novice process users. This method promotes procedures for experienced users and work instructions for novice users. The software process model method also recognizes that portions of your business require just low-level instructions

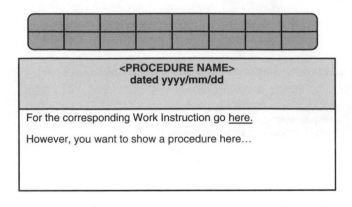

Figure 12.8   Procedure header Web page.

(e.g., a manufacturing environment). In these instances, you may want only a work instruction and no procedure. The how selector should make this clear. Conversely, engineering how-to process elements tend to be procedures and not work instructions. This software process approach has total flexibility to address the variations needed in businesses.

USING THE SOFTWARE PROCESS MODEL

Chapter 13

Users of the Software Process Model

Classes of Customers Using This Model

To get an overall feel for the software process model, we need to look at the parts of this process model that are the most applicable to different classes of process customers:

- The general customer
- The line/project management customer
- The lead/practitioner customer
- The quality/process-group customer

The specified parts are not mutually exclusive to each type of customer. Each part certainly has a predominant use for a particular class of customer.

General Customer

All people who have any connection with or are users of the process framework architecture will use the following parts:

- Training — side 2
  - Software process model method overview
  - Process intranet training

- Standards/maturity model/regulations compliance awareness training
■ General time-card charging method related to the process activities (only if your time-card system supports this process connection)

General customers would be candidates for new-hire orientation training (or employee transfer training) in addition to any standard human resources–type of orientation training. Everyone needs this training once the software process framework architecture is in place.

Line/Project Management Customer

Because line management and project management personnel are involved in project planning for estimation, project tracking for planned versus actuals, and project execution for earned value, the following parts of the process model are particularly important to this class of customer:

■ Repeatable level — side 1:
  - End-to-end life-cycle diagram
  - Process activity diagrams (PADs) within that end-to-end life cycle
■ Support level — side 1:
  - Activity actuals (for future estimations, but only if the time-card charging system cannot get this)
■ Training — side 2:
  - End-to-end life-cycle training (including PADs)
  - Activity overview training
  - Project planning training with this software process method
  - Project tracking training with this software process method
  - Project metrics training with this software process method

The practitioners rarely need to look at the repeatable-level items mentioned above except perhaps their own functional PADs. Only responsible people shown on schedule tasks (activity instances) need to add data to the support-level item if the time-card charging system doesn't map to this process methodology. Leads may find overview (or awareness) training helpful for project planning and tracking — but only at the cursory level.

Lead/Practitioner Customer

Because leads and practitioners are involved in the real process work, the following parts of the process model are particularly important to this class of customer:

- Repeatable level — side 1:
  - PADs for their own functional areas
  - Activities
- Implementation level — side 1:
  - How selectors
  - Procedures and work instructions
- Support level — side 1:
  - Work product selectors
  - Work product sets
  - Form selectors
  - Form sets
  - Activity actuals (for future estimations — for leads only and only if the time-card charging system cannot get this)
- Training — side 2:
  - End-to-end life-cycle training (including PADs)
  - Activity overview training
  - Specific life-cycle PAD "swim lane" training (e.g., software engineering)
  - Inspection procedure training
  - Configuration management (CM) interface training from activities
  - Specific functional area training (e.g., requirements management — for those who need it)

Quality/Process-Group Customer

Quality and process-group customers certainly need an overall knowledge of the entire process repository. They do not need to have intimate knowledge of all process elements — particularly those that are domain-specific. I would expect this class of customer to really know the inspection procedure, configuration management procedural "hooks" from any activity, and metrics-collection aspects of this model. These are common to all activities and have universal applicability. I would also expect this class of customer to have awareness knowledge of all process elements. For these reasons, the level of training is really a superset of all training with particular emphasis on the following topics:

- Repeatable level — side 1:
  - PADs relevant to their own "swim lane" if pertinent
  - Activities
- Implementation level — side 1:
  - How selectors
  - Procedures and work instructions
- Support level — side 1:
  - Work product selectors
  - Work product sets
  - Form selectors
  - Form sets
- Training — side 2:
  - End-to-end life-cycle training (including PADs)
  - Activity overview training
  - Specific functional area PAD "swim lane" training (e.g., software engineering — at an awareness level)
  - Inspection procedure training
  - Configuration management (CM) interface training from activities

Chapter 14

Metrics Collection Using This Software Process Model

Metrics Collection versus Presentation

There is a wise saying that says, "You can't improve what you can't measure." The software process model is very cognizant of the importance of metrics data collection and metrics information presentation. I make a distinction between metrics "data" and metrics "information." Metrics data is not that interesting but is a snapshot of a target area of interest. Metrics information is the summation or trends of that metrics data in a form that is useful to the viewer. That informational form could be a pie graph, a bar chart, a scatter chart, or a table. Metrics data is that which is collected as a byproduct of an activity execution using this software process model. Metrics information is a work product produced either by a metrics-related event-driven procedure or a schedulable activity.

Metrics Data Collection

Metrics data collection follows the same premise at the very essence of this process model — i.e., separate "what you need to do" from "how you are to do it." Metrics data collection is a "what you have to do" item that is built into each and every activity that requires metrics data collection. Each activity is made up of a small set of high-level steps that you absolutely, positively want done. One of the final steps that is advocated in this software process model is the "End" step in all activities. The "End" step is there to:

- Notify various roles that this activity has been executed and is "done." As stated before, these roles could include:
  - The next activity leads shown in the project schedule
  - The project manager
  - The development manager
  - The scheduling folks for "earned value"
  - The accounting folks for charge number elaborations.
  - SCM for expansion of the developmental repository.
- If this activity is designated as an activity that has metrics data collection involved, then this same step notifies the metrics group (and passes on) metrics data. In your organization, a "metrics group" could be:
  - A discrete metrics presentation group
  - Your quality organization
  - Your process group

There is much to be said for a discrete group responsible for receiving metrics data and turning it into useful information. These folks should be skilled in graphical representation of that metrics data.

If you have a complex metrics data–collection procedure, I recommend that you include a high-level step within that activity as an important how-to anchor for that metrics collection procedural world. Like all other how-to procedures and procedural elements, any how-to goes through a how selector. The software process model treats any metrics-collection how-to like any other how-to.

Metrics Information Presentation

Metrics information presentation can be:

- An event-driven procedure when metrics information is asynchronous in nature
- An activity on your project schedule when metrics information is schedulable on a periodic calendar

There is much to be said for creating a process element for metrics presentation. Like other process elements in this software process model, you get to hyperlink to the metrics work product via a work product selector. This follows the model for metrics just like any other work product, in that it:

- Allows for metrics work product variability via selection
- Allows for metrics work product templates
- Allows for metrics work product inspection checklists
- Allows for metrics work product guidelines
- Allows for metrics work product example(s)

This software process model is good at getting rid of any ambiguities by using the selectability built into the model to specific end items.

If you are gathering metrics data on an asynchronous basis but producing metrics information presentations on a scheduled basis, you will want an activity on your schedule that converts the metrics data into useful information. If you do this correctly, you will place this metrics-based activity in the swim lane for your support folks versus the main engineering swim lane. It makes it adamantly clear that there are linkages from mainstream activities to this one. It also shows that this particular activity is a support-type activity. The software process model handles this very well on a practical level and at a visual level.

Chapter 15

Schedule Management Using This Software Process Model

Schedule Planning versus Execution

Before going further, I really want to differentiate between planning a schedule and executing a schedule. These are two separate things. I mention this because I have run into my fair share of project managers who have not understood this! They have mistakenly mapped out a planned (estimated) schedule and then held people's feet to the fire when executing that schedule! They seem to feel that a planned schedule is "set in concrete" for execution rather than an execution estimation. Sometimes an estimate is just that and does not reflect reality. You may estimate 50 units to be coded in a subsystem and at execution time, that number is 57. If you were that close for estimation, I'd be a happy camper as a project manager! I saw a project manager throw a fit over this discrepancy and force the actual number to be as estimated — even though it was wrong. The project manager had erroneously tried to map the actual execution schedule story to the estimation schedule story. This skewed view of schedules caused bad products just to placate this project manager's tirade.

The intersection of these two worlds is where you use the estimating schedule as a planning baseline and compare the execution actual mapping to that baseline. When an execution schedule starts out, all future planned events are planning packages from the planning schedule. As execution progresses, we replace the planning packages of the planning schedule with the actual execution activity instances (tasks). At any given point in time, you have the real picture of process activity instances and yet-to-do planning packages from the planning schedule. When the project execution is totally done, all the planning packages of the original planning schedule have been replaced with actual activity (task) instances showing what actually happened.

Schedule Planning

Planning schedules can be done quite easily using this process framework architecture by:

- Estimating the parts story
- Estimating the integration planning story
- Mapping the appropriate activities on your planning schedule to match that estimation
- Adding in the prior actuals for resources
- Rolling up to summary line items for duration and costs

The parts estimation story gives you the basic building blocks for mapping out the planning schedule. For example, if you estimate that you have three subsystems to be designed for your system, you know you have something like Figure 15.1 on your planning schedule.

You know you have a system-level design activity. You know you have three subsystem designs to do. If you know these are totally separate teams, then the subsystem designs can be truly concurrent — as shown. If the people resources are limited, these subsystem designs need to be somewhat serial in nature rather than concurrent.

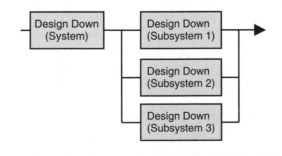

Figure 15.1 Estimation snippet.

If you estimate 50 units for subsystem 1, 75 units for subsystem 2, and 100 units for subsystem 3, then you have a tremendous amount of planning knowledge to map all these out. If you estimate that 20 percent of the units are reused coding, you know that you just need to integrate those units and that's it. *Use the software process model to create that planning schedule.*

If you estimate that you need a foundation of work done in subsystem 1 for anything else to be tested, that would give you a strong clue that you need a foundation integration-type of activity. If you estimate ten other integration sets, then you know you have ten integration activities to plan.

At this point, all planning activities are presumed to be of equal duration, etc. You now replace the default duration with actuals from previous work. At this stage, you can replace the defaults with averages for estimation purposes. You can also do resource loading on your planning schedule to make sure that you're not overbooking people.

With normal scheduling rollups, you can now estimate the total project schedule for duration and costs by just using this software process model. If you're smart, you will compare this with other estimation techniques like function points or lines of code to get a sanity check on these estimates.

The key to planning a schedule is to:

- Use the activity PADs to get to that end-to-end planning story first. You use past experience or rough design to arrive at the parts story and map that to the process world shown in each PAD.
- Place the atomic activities on the planning schedule following the predecessor/successor rules in each PAD. This provides the basis or underlying foundation to all your planning packages.
- Use the software process model's activity groups by part and roll up the activities to create the high-level planning packages. Planning packages, by definition, are high-level and reflect roll-ups of lower-level details. In the software process model, the lower-level details are at the activity level. You will also find it useful to have multiple layers of roll-ups. For example, "Subsystem A Design" may represent the first roll-up while that planning package along with "Subsystem B Design" can be further rolled up to "Subsystems Design." Note that planning packages are noun-based in this model whereas activities are verb-based, indicating an action.
- Use the roll-ups as the planning schedule and hide the supporting activity details. You will need the supporting details afterward for that important sanity check at postmortem time to ratify schedule estimates versus schedule actuals.

In summary, use the software process model to do a bottoms-up development of your planning packages. As we execute a schedule, we do exactly the same with real schedule tasks.

Schedule Execution

For those of you who have project management experience, this section will be very different from what you have done before. *Don't put work package tasks on a schedule until you absolutely know that they are to exist.* This means that you do not place tasks on a schedule unless the model or model execution tells you to do this. Project managers get very nervous about not laying the whole thing out all at once. I am saying the opposite — you treat the schedule as you would for spiral development. For software spiral development, you design a little, code a little, etc. In this model, you do exactly the same except the model itself calls the shots on schedule tasking.

How do you know when they are to exist? I am making the claim that several things provide that direction:

- The process end-to-end activity diagrams in the model provide the predecessor/successor relationships allowable on any schedule as a foundation.
- The execution of design decomposition types of activities not only provides further visibility on the design but also identifies elaboration threads for schedule execution. For example, a completed execution of a system-level design activity lets you know exactly how many subsystems you have. A completed execution of a subsystem design activity lets you know exactly how many units you have. In this software process model you drive the execution schedule from this known information.
- The execution of any activity that creates or updates the integration plan provides the integration strategy for the project schedule. The same integration plan also provides marvelous insight into which implementations can be prioritized for just-in-time integrations. This is why I consider the integration plan to be the most important plan in the life cycle. You not only know the road map to the parts but you also know what items can be deferred to achieve major cost savings for time-to-market.

The combinations of these factors provide the project manager with the identification of *what* activities to place on a schedule and *when* to place them on a schedule. Any execution schedule that is developed using this software process model reflects absolute reality at all times!

At various points in a schedule life cycle, the project manager will need to reconcile the work packages (actual work performed) with the planning packages (planned or estimated work to be performed). The ideal situation is to have the actuals be close to what was estimated. If they are far apart, use this opportunity to determine the reasons why you have this discrepancy. As you use this model, you will find that you can collect actuals over time that will produce better and better estimates for future projects.

When you align all the project management scheduling with this process model, you get a powerful connection of processes to the real world. When you further align your time-card reporting system to that same process model, the whole world of powerful metrics opens up related to both the target product for estimations and actuals and to process improvement.

I make a huge connection of activity instances to project schedules. You may conclude that I am also suggesting that project schedules cover high-level summaries all the way down to individual task items per unit to be coded. But the level of detail that you want in your main project schedules is up to you. A user-friendly project management tool is ideal to provide a selected granularity of that project's schedule where low-level task elements naturally roll up to higher-level elements and so on. Several companies where I have worked made a conscious separation of project line items as follows:

- High-level representation for the project manager and senior management (typically done using a project management tool)
- Low-level representation for the lead to manage (typically done with a simple table or spreadsheet)

I must admit that the driving force for this separation (with accompanying disconnects) was rooted in the tool being unwieldy and not suitable for this. People get real good at work-arounds even though the ideal is to not do work-arounds but deal with the tool issue directly. A bad side issue in separation is that you can produce serious disconnects (i.e., which form do you believe?). For that reason, I advocate using a single scheduling tool and hiding the level of detail needed as appropriate. You maintain schedule integrity that way.

Whether you place all schedule tasks in one tool or not, this model still pushes for that direct connection of process activities. You still want to get earned value on any activity instance completion no matter how you show work to be done.

Chapter 16

Project Estimation Using This Software Process Model

General Project Estimation

This is the one topic that can make or break any company. If you are not good at project cost estimation, you may lose your shirt pricing things! Conversely, if you really understand your costs, you can price your work to be profitable. This software process model is very aware of and supportive of gaining the following estimation data:

- Financial costs
- Durations
- Resources
- Special needs (e.g., labs, training)

Having worked in the DoD contracting business for many years, I know that the days of putting in low bids to get work and then adjusting costs later have long gone. I worked at one place where the submitted bid was so out-of-bed with costs that the company lost a ton of money. I realize that there are times when you might want to purposely have a "loss leader" to:

- Expand your customer base
- Get inroads into some industry
- Cultivate a particular important customer
- Introduce a new product, etc.

This decision should be made with your eyes wide open — not as an estimation surprise.

The software process model supports two ways of providing that important estimation data. You can use one or both as adjuncts to each other:

- A runtime postactivity explicit manual act by the activity lead:
  - Upside: You can capture experience levels of your people resources involved for any given activity.
  - Upside: You can capture actual activity duration.
  - Upside: You can record special circumstances and notes pertinent to any estimate.
  - Downside: It is manual and requires the discipline of each activity lead to document these kinds of things.
  - Downside: It requires explicit data extraction by named parts as determined by your organization.
- A byproduct of your time-charging system that uses the software process model:
  - Upside: True actual costs are by activity.
  - Upside: True duration is by activity.
  - Upside: True actual resources used are by activity.
  - Upside: True part costs breakdown is by activity.
  - Upside: Data can be retrieved at will at any time.
  - Downside: It can only relate real people's names — not classes of experience levels.
  - Downside: It cannot capture special circumstances or notes pertinent to any actual — unless schedule variances are used for that purpose.

Please note that I qualified the time-card charging system as one that uses this method. The ideal situation is when your time-card charging is totally aligned with the software process model's activities. (See the following chapter on time-card charging for a suggested approach to achieve this goal.)

I have worked at companies that have gone to great lengths to come up with a standardized work breakdown structure (WBS) for scheduling. The trouble is that you can end up with a WBS that is not aligned with this activity-based process model. The ideal WBS has a direct mapping of activities to WBS line items. Another way of saying this is that if you do this right, activity group names can be inferred as your WBS line items. If you achieve this mapping, you now have a powerful mapping of your process world to your WBS world.

Manual Estimation by Activity Lead

You can do this regardless of your time-card system. It works the best when used in conjunction with your process model–based time-card charging system. I found that the best approach for collecting manual estimates was by important parts of your system. The level of granularity should be at the level of your components that could be reused or are marketed at that level. For most companies, the subsystem level is appropriate. For those companies that are in the lower-level component business, component units might be more appropriate.

One commercial company had organized the software labor pool by subsystem. Because of this division, each subsystem had a subsystem lead in charge of that part of the system. You can do this only if the subsystems are well defined and relatively static. For that commercial company, this organization worked well by having subsystem expertise concentrated in that subsystem group. In that environment, collecting estimations at the subsystem level made a lot of sense. The subsystem lead had a vested interest in collecting estimation data pertinent to his or her subsystem.

In the DoD contracting environment, this doesn't work as well unless you have a high degree of reusable software components in different contracts. Most companies talk about reusability, but they seldom achieve any degree of true reuse. In this climate, each project (or contract) has a project manager. This organization works against reuse because project managers do not want additional costs on their watch for the good of the enterprise. Having said all this, it is still reasonable to collect estimation data by parts because all delivered systems are made up of parts. Unlike the commercial environment above, more pressure is on each activity lead to "do the right thing" related to capturing estimation data. There is no subsystem lead to enforce this. The project manager is typically not interested in this at all and prefers it not be done on his or her dime.

Having said all this, how does the software process model help to do all this data capture to aid future estimations? Here's how this works:

- Each activity has a small set of high-level steps with certain high-level steps in all activities.
- One mandated step is for the activity lead to execute the "End" step.

■ In addition to notifying various roles on being "done" and passing metrics off to the metrics group, this step could be used to add capturing actual data for future estimations.

■ Collect actuals and notes in a file associated with the activity object as shown on the schedule. If you are coding a unit within a subsystem, you capture actuals by activity names in that subsystem's estimation file. You can do this because this model can associate any activity to a part.

When you think about it, this is an ideal time to capture this type of information because it's fresh in the activity lead's mind.

At "End" time, the activity lead:

■ Looks at the activity object on the schedule
■ Relates the object to the appropriate part
■ Goes to the collection container file for that part (a hyperlink to the set of files would be useful here)
■ Goes down to the activity section of this collection file
■ Fills in information that will help future estimations:
    – How many people worked that activity
    – Makeup of the group (novices, experienced, etc.)
    – Duration of the activity
    – Lowest and highest estimations depending on whether experienced workers, novices, or a mixture were used for that estimation
    – Special notes

The lowest and highest piece of data will be very useful for future estimations because it came from the activity lead involved. On future projects, the project manager will be able to take this activity-based data and project estimates when developing the lower-level foundations to get to the planning packages. If you know you have a bad resource situation from before, use the pessimistic data as the estimate. If you have a richer resource situation, use the optimistic data as the estimate.

Every time an activity lead executes his or her activity against any particular part of the system, you will add to the actuals database for future estimations. Over time, you will be able to normalize this estimation data to compensate for optimistic activity leads versus pessimistic activity leads. In other words, your estimations will get better and better over time. Also, the estimates are activity based within a part and are totally aligned with the software process model.

The beauty of this approach is that you can take any part of your system and determine the set of activities that could have that part as an activity object on a schedule. Once you determine the granularity of your collection files, you create one file per selected part. You then include a section for each activity name within that file. These files could be Word files.

On one implementation, I simply pointed all activities to that list of files and had the activity lead determine which one applied. You can do this quicker by just pointing to a subset list of files where this activity can apply. The software process model can be that flexible.

Chapter 17

Time-Card Charging Using This Software Process Model

You want to get to the point where your time-card reporting system is totally aligned with this process approach. You want people to charge to a number that ties the work performed to the execution of activity instances on a schedule.

A charge number is made up of:

- A project identification part
- The WBS structure
- Rework indicator of null

For schedulable WBS elements, the breakdown is further subdivided into:

- Activity being worked
- Object of the activity being worked followed by a rework counter

Nonschedulable WBS elements have no rework counter (i.e., null) since these items tend to be equipment, software, lab costs, etc.

Let's look at the hierarchy of information that you need on a time-card charge number for schedulable work:

- *Project being worked*. This should be a predetermined list of possibilities. This list is mostly static with revisions as needed for new projects added and old projects dropped.
- *Activity being worked*. This is the specific activity (within the project) from the activity pick list that now shows up as a schedule instance. This list is virtually static with changes occurring only when new activities are added in the process world.
- *Object of the activity being worked*. This object can be a part identifier or a test set. The part list is derived directly from the project's design decomposition activities. The part list is project-specific and can certainly reflect the indentured parts list for any given system. The test set is derived directly from the project's integration plan. The test sets are project-specific.*
- *Activity rework counter*. This is merely a zero (original effort) versus a non-zero (rework effort) tacked on the time-card charge number. The non-zero number is circular from 1...9 and back to 1.

For nonschedulable work, the time card number breakdown is:

- Project being worked. This is the same as before.
- Zeros. An "activity" of all zeros indicates all the nonschedulable aspect of the WBS.
- All the nonschedulable line items. It is beyond the scope of this book to describe these other than the state that these are static line items.
- A null rework counter. The focus of this book is on the schedulable charge number method.

---

* We use this process model's design and planning work products to not only feed into the target life cycle but also to use the information directly for project management purposes. I'm only establishing the known parts up front and allowing the project's design itself to elaborate on subsequent parts. This is a radical departure from traditional charge-number schemes. My approach is to expand the parts list, as we know for sure that they are to exist. We don't second-guess this list at all. We use the same technique for integration set objects. We wait until our integration plan spells what these integration sets are and then we include them in our time-card charging method. If you haven't realized it yet, I am using design decompositions and plans to also manage the project via activities and time charging. Historically, plans were things that the customer wanted and you produced them because you had to contractually. I'm using these plans to drive the project via process activities. What a concept! I'm also using design decompositions to drive the project via process activities — beyond actually externalizing a design. This is a veritable two-for-one sale. In this model, plans and designs are real and actually utilized.

I will map all this out onto a hypothetical nine-digit charge-number system as follows:

PPAAOOOOR

Where

PP	= Project identifier
AA	= Activity identifier
OOOO	= Activity object. Part or test set identifier for project PP above
R	= Rework counter 0…9

For project "03," all charge numbers would start with "03." If the "Design Down" activity was identified as "07," then all charge numbers of this particular activity would start with "0307." If the system was identified as "10" and the 3 subsystems were identified as "11," "12," and "13" respectively, then for people doing those designs, they would charge to "030710" for top-level system design, "030711" for subsystem #1 design, "030712" for subsystem #2 design, and finally, "030713" for subsystem #3 design. Zeros are filled out to normalize your total charge number. You place a zero at the end when you do this design for the first time. If you have to do this design again, you place a 1 at the end. If you have to do it yet again, you place a 2 at the end, etc. Rework happens due to two major events:

■ Customer-driven changes requiring schedule rework
■ Process deficiencies requiring schedule rework

The former cannot be controlled; however, the latter indicates serious process issues that need to be addressed. When you get customer-driven changes, you need to "prune" one or more branches of a schedule "tree" of activities and rework them. When you do that, the charge number for each activity is the same as before but with a rework counter (non-zero) at the end. If you are forced to rework activities on a schedule due to process problems, this is a huge red flag to your process group to analyze and fix the process problem so that you don't have this rework showing up again.

With this charge-number scheme being tied into process activities, you can readily get metrics on a variety of things:

■ All project PP charges by querying the PPxxxxxxx portion of the charge number
■ All specific activity charges for activity AA across all projects by querying the xxAAxxxxx portion of the charge number

- All specific activity charges for activity AA for project PP by querying the PPAAxxxxx portion of the charge number
- Analysis/design/code/test view for project PP by querying all the PPAAxxxxx portions that make up that view
- All charges for a particular part of the indentured parts list (for example, all costs related to a subsystem identified by object "13xx" within project PP can be achieved by querying the PPxx13xxx portion of the charge number)
- All rework costs for project PP by querying the PPxxxxxxN portion of the charge number where "N" is not zero

In addition, because activities belong to activity groups, you can create pie charts showing the percentage effort spent on analysis versus design versus coding versus testing, etc. You can now compare your actuals with industry standards to find out how you stand relative to your competition!

From a process improvement perspective, you can create Pareto charts showing activities along one side and execution time along the other to determine where your time is being spent! Because schedule tasks come from an activity pick list, we can now do this. Just like dynamic analyzers of coding, we can determine which activity is used the most on a schedule and the amount of time spent doing that activity in total. You can readily see that a small process improvement in the most used activity will produce enormous results. Pareto analysis will direct you to the activity of interest for process improvement. After tackling the topmost activity, you can tackle the next–most used activity, etc. If you execute a single system design activity but execute the "implement" activity 2,000 times, a small change in the "implement" activity has a large impact. You will actually be able to shorten your life-cycle costs and reduce your time-to-market for any product by focusing on your process elements.

In general, processes of interest to optimize are:

- All procedural elaborations of the common activity high-level steps — particularly the inspection procedure
- Highest instance count of any activity as determined by a Pareto chart

Chapter 18

Subcontract Management Using This Software Process Model

Subcontractor Management Components

There is an incredible aspect of this software process model relating to subcontract management.

Certainly, in the DoD contracting world, the prime contractor can be required to flow down certain things to a subcontractor. Process is usually high on the requirement for flow-down.

Subcontractor management involves:

- Supplier selection
- Supplier agreement management

It is no accident that the CMMI covers both of these topics as capability model process areas (PAs). The former deals with how you go about selecting your subcontractors whereas the latter deals with managing subcontractors once they are onboard. This process model addresses both of these PAs very nicely.

You need to check out subcontractors ahead of time (supplier selection, or SS) and you need to manage them as they execute the terms of the subcontract (supplier agreement management, or SAM).

Supplier Selection

Sometimes international proposals require in-country subcontractors where that first level of selection is predetermined by the foreign government. At an extreme, the prime contractor may be told what in-country subcontractor to select — which effectively negates the SS portion. Most of the time, you are in charge of selecting and managing subcontractors.

If you are truly in the SS business, you will need to determine these things:

- Validation of the supplier as a potential subcontractor (i.e., are they in the right business?)
- Can they perform in the proposed time frame?
- Where are they for their processes? (i.e., what is their process maturity?)

These questions often require an onsite visit and audit.

As a rule, you don't want a subcontractor who has no track record of producing on-time quality products. If their deliverable target is part of your delivered target to the customer, you don't want a failure traced to the subcontracted part. That's where process comes in.

Let's turn our attention to how this process framework architecture helps supplier selection. The software process model helps in the following areas:

- You can establish a complete mini–life cycle of activities in the preproposal section of your life cycle specifically addressing subcontractor selection. This eliminates any ambiguity as to what is needed.
- You can provide a predetermined list of approved suppliers referenced from activities within this mini–life cycle for both domestic and foreign subcontractors. These are preapproved based on process maturity and market niche products.
- Like all other activities, you can associate how-to selections via how selectors from these activities. Variations related to parts suppliers versus service suppliers are readily handled by the software process model approach.
- You can provide the subcontractor with a list of schedulable activities and end-to-end processes early for them to connect their own procedural how-tos (and tool-set differences) to these activities. The what–how separation of this software process model provides tremendous portability at the "what" level (activities) while allowing a plug-and-play for their how-to elaborations. This allows

for subcontractor configuration management differences and yet requires CM control equivalents based on work products. This early visibility for the subcontractor provides them with a real-world road map for process compliance.

■ You can provide quality inspection checklists on specific work products early. This software process model specifies acceptance criteria for delivered work products that are "done." This acceptance criterion is identical for internal suppliers as it is for external suppliers. This model supports quality audits because quality gates are built into the process approach. Although used at execution time, it is desirable to let your subcontractors know upfront how acceptance will be performed on all work products.

■ You can provide the mini–life cycle for SS to the subcontractor to allow that subcontractor to meet or exceed any stated requirements.

Supplier Agreement Management

When you have an agreed-upon contract with your customer, you now need to pay attention to managing any and all subcontractors during execution of this contract.

I want to make a big point about the software process model and its treatment of parts to be ultimately delivered to the customer. If you did this right, you would have a macro-level picture of the deliverable parts as a result of the proposal process. Think about the totality of all parts as a big pie that is cut up into slices. Some slices are done in-house and some are done by subcontracted labor. From a schedule and project management perspective, you don't care what color badges people are wearing to do work — you just want quality work performed on or before time. Your schedules need to show all parts involved in the whole pie — no matter who is working on them.

Regardless of the particular slice of work, you have dependencies involved — such as people resources and work product availability. This is no difference for slices marked for subcontracting versus slices done in-house. Your schedules should reflect these predecessor/successor relationships no matter what.

This is where the process model shines:

■ The basic what–how separation provides both a pick list of schedulable activities and an end-to-end representation of those activities showing predecessor/successor relationships. When following this software process model, the project schedule reflects instances of these same activities — regardless of who does what. You flow down the activities to your subcontractors. You don't flow down your procedural elaborations. They (the subcontractors) provide their own ways (or how-tos) of doing things.

■ The project manager can choose to track subcontractor progress at the same level as internal employees or can choose to track subcontractors at a higher level, with the subcontractors themselves tracking at the same level as internal employees. The model supports both notions. No matter what, all progress (and thus earned value) is based on the identical activities — whether they are done in-house or by subcontractors.

■ Each software process model activity requires all high-level steps to be done. There is no distinction between an activity assigned to a subcontractor versus an activity assigned to an in-house lead. All steps are auditable. Audits can be done by anyone. No work product can be promoted to the next activity without quality inspection records to signify "done." That is just as true for a subcontractor as it is for an in-house lead.

■ Configuration management is built into the process model — including levels of control based on an individual work product and phase. The identical requirements are levied on all activities being executed — whether in-house or subcontracted. Because of this aspect of the process model, CM is totally auditable.

■ Metrics data collection is built into the process model. The identical requirements are levied on all activities being executed where metrics are called out — whether in-house or subcontracted. Because of this aspect of the process model, metrics data collection is totally auditable — no matter where the activity is executed.

The software process model makes no distinction with the "who does what" question. The model recognizes that we need acceptance criteria for all work products — regardless of the "who" question. This fundamental notion makes subcontract management no different from in-house team management. If you manage one, you manage both. We want producers of work products to be accountable for quality.

Chapter 19

Integrated Teams Using This Software Process Model

Integrated Teaming Concepts

This is a topic that warrants some discussion. When companies use the term "integrated," it can mean many things to many people — such as:

- A team composed of different disciplines necessary to achieve a stated effort or goal. A surgical team comes to mind as a real world example. This team is totally integrated, with different people taking different roles.
- A team composed of a single predominant discipline that has access to other disciplines as needed to achieve a stated effort or goal. A process group comes to mind as a real-world example, where "process people" bring in domain specialists as needed via subordinate process action teams to solve specific process problems.
- One or the other of the above, but with customer involvement as part of the integration. Large DoD contracts sometimes specify these types of teams — usually called integrated product teams. The idea here is that the customer is represented throughout and thus has ongoing visibility into all aspects of the developmental life cycle.

In all instances, we have the situation where different roles are involved to get work done. To be effective, you need to make sure there's a high level of communication between these different roles so that the left hand knows what the right hand is doing.

You can complicate accomplishing any form of integrated team by how the company is organized. Product-based functional organizations may not have (or control) all the necessary disciplines needed to support this notion. Matrix-type organizations may not be able to support all matrix demands as well. Some companies have a mix-and-match of matrix groups for technical stuff (e.g., software engineers) and a cadre of corporate groups (e.g., technical publications) that become additional matrix organizations for other nontechnical stuff.

Add the process world to all this. If you have processes as follows, you are at odds with any kind of successful integrated teaming:

- Stovepiped processes by functional area or department. This provides a total disconnect between disciplines and roles beyond the stovepipe.
- Process elements that are "owned" by a function within the company. Multiple process owners are a clue that you have a problem.
- Process elements that do not address or recognize the importance of multiple roles in an end product. Roles connectivity to tasks may or may not exist.
- Process elements created in a vacuum with no connectivity to other process elements — which is key to deterministic handoffs and interfaces.
- Lack of communication steps in your process elements — which is a key ingredient to integrated teaming.

The software process model is excellent for integrated teams because:

- Activities have a built-in notion that multiple roles can be involved in each and every step. The software process method discourages the notion of stovepiping process elements by organizational element.
- Work products are data that flow between activities and are well defined — no matter who executes the receiving activity.
- Roles can be predetermined for each and every activity, thus solidifying successful teaming arrangements.

- Software process model inspections encourage work product consumer involvement as part of the inspection team. This includes both internal and external customer involvement as necessary. For key deliverables, the external customer (or designated representative) can readily be included in the inspection process.
- The software process model activity is the atomic process element for earned value. That same activity team can readily be an integrated team to support the stated roles.

DEPLOYING THE SOFTWARE PROCESS MODEL

Chapter 20

Deployment Foundation Issues

Establish Key Roles/Charter for Deployment

The very first order of business is to firmly establish "who's on first" for getting deployment done. Senior management is crucial at this point for making sure all their direct reports and managers are on board with this and that it comes from the top. I mention this because at one place I worked, we immediately got into interdepartment squabbling due to a lack of senior management support and direction. If you hear a manager say things like "do what you want — but don't touch my area," you will have deployment problems.

I strongly recommend the formation of a process group as the focal point for all matters related to process and process deployment. This group has to have both the authorization and responsibility for process. If you have a distributed set of "process owners," consolidate that responsibility and authority to this new group. My requirements for membership in this process group are:

- *Six to eight people.* Larger process groups tend to be less efficient and more cumbersome. A smaller group tends to be ineffective. It is not necessary to have representatives from all corners of your organization. It is important that these domain experts get called in as necessary for process development and inspection. One company had a 15-person process group established by a non–process-oriented vice president. It was a disaster to get a repeatable quorum present for any meeting. We spent subsequent meetings repeating stuff from earlier meetings to accommodate a different set of participants at every meeting.

■ *Process-group commitments.* My most successful process group was when I insisted that members commit 5 percent of their workweek to process-group meetings. Group members and their managers had to sign the commitment. The 5 percent figure is doable — even for busy people. Two one-hour meetings per week reflect that percentage. I also had fixed time meetings both by time and day of week. It became automatic to show up. To make this really work, I was the process-group lead and I dedicated 100 percent to this effort. I had clerical support services available to me. The most effective process-group meetings are concentrated sessions with a time-stamped agenda and where my support staff and I do all extracurricular activities. You want to restrict extra time (beyond actual process-group meeting time) needed by your key process participants because they tend to be super busy.

■ *Showing up on time.* We could not tolerate people wandering in five or ten minutes late. We started promptly on the hour and stopped promptly on the hour. At one company, I removed a person for being late because it held everyone up. Promptness became so important at one commercial company that other process-group members would be "all over" tardy people. The tardiness stopped quickly when peers got involved in any discipline.

■ *People who are process oriented.* Do not have people in this group who don't fit this requirement! At one company, a vice president insisted on naming people to the group (which became double the size I had wanted) who were almost completely ignorant about process. We spent almost all our precious process-group time just getting these people to understand the most fundamental aspects of process. It was painful. The VP wondered why progress was slow. Duh!

■ *People who are opinionated — i.e., not afraid to speak up on issues.* You cannot afford to have people just show up and suck air out of the room and not participate. The best processes I've developed came from sessions where it was not clear who would walk out alive after spirited process discussions.

■ *People that others look up to.* They may be leads or workers. Every organization has these types of people and they may not be in the management ranks. The reason for this requirement is to form an initial set of process champions right out of the box. These initial process champions will develop more champions.

■ *People who are willing to have an enterprise perspective versus an organizational perspective.* This could be a huge problem if process-group discussions degenerate into preservation of turf — no matter what. At one place, I actually went to a paint store, bought disposable painting hats, placed a big "E" for enterprise on the hats, and made process-group members wear the hats at our meetings to reinforce that enterprise focus. It got a few laughs and some grumbles but it worked.

■ *People who are not "who" oriented.* A process group avoids the "who" question and concentrates on the "whats." Once the "what you have to do" is addressed, the "who" looks after itself. When process-group meetings degenerated into discussing "who does this" and "who does that," I routinely stopped the meeting and reminded everyone that when you have a hole in the bottom of the boat, this is not the time to discuss whose hole it is! I got laughs but my point was taken.

This is your key group for process development and deployment.

It's obvious, but if you have this marvelous group put together without regard to an overall process architectural goal, you will fail. This is where this software process model will help you enormously. Ideally, the process-group lead has an in-depth knowledge of the targeted process architecture with an initial goal to get the process group up to speed on this aspect first — before any company processes are tackled. If you are under pressure to "just get on with it" (without getting all process members up on the target process architecture), you will fail. You will end up flailing around for a large amount of time. You will also end up with a hodgepodge of process elements and no encompassing architecture.

You want to end up with a hierarchy of goals supported by tasks that are measurable for earned value and progress reporting by the process group itself. Essentially, you want to create a balanced scorecard for process progress. This makes your process group accountable for progress just like any other project team.

For deployment success, I will repeat an important division of labor within the process group itself. You absolutely need to develop advocates for the process framework architecture itself and make sure the integrity of the process model is maintained. This book will be invaluable for that aspect. These people are very different from most process-group members, who should be domain experts. The process framework advocates are the folks that put the "meat on the bone" for process and they will make sure that the process parts all fit within that framework architecture, whereas the domain folks make sure to develop process elements that are useful and make sense.

I make this point because uneducated management personnel may pressure you to "just get on with it" without considering the importance of making sure that all process elements fit within a framework architecture. The worst thing you can do is crank out process into an ever larger pile of stuff that increasingly gets more and more useless for the organization. The main litmus test for process is that it is useful. I have run into managers who seem to think that bigger piles mean success. In reality, you may have just the opposite result. Resist those who are pushing you in that direction for success.

The most successful process group I led was when I was not only the lead but also the process architect and had management backing to do what was needed. I mention management backing because at another place, I had the exact same situation but had a boss who was so insecure that all my suggestions and recommendations were either ignored or rejected because they didn't come from him! Anything from me was dead on arrival. If you're ever in that position, run, don't walk! You cannot succeed. There are people like that out there and (sadly) some are in senior management positions. I simply didn't want to manipulate him to have him believe that all ideas were his ideas. That's what it would take to deal with this kind of person.

Ensure an Inspection Procedure Is in Place

When actually doing process deployment for the software process model, there is one how-to procedure that absolutely needs to be addressed early on: the inspection procedure. This particular procedure is fundamental to all the activities within this software process model as a quality gate. If you have a lousy how-to procedure here, you will have an awful time in getting people to buy into this model. Conversely, a good how-to will take off like wildfire and become engrained in an organization real fast. The software process model wants quality built in the "what you have to do" world by placing the quality responsibility on the producer's back. The inspection procedure is critical to this end goal.

I worked at one place that had a "review" procedure in place. It was hardly used, did not work well, and the management protected it with their lives. I had the gall to suggest a better way of doing things. I had to present this new way at three different hearings to this management group, finally receiving a disposition of "rejected." They could not handle the fact that this software process model allows for better mousetraps. Both methods could coexist in this model. I knew that once the better way was an option, the bad way would drop off for usage very naturally. These managers had a personal and vested interest in preserving the status quo — regardless of usefulness. They had invested time in the existing process element. They wanted no interlopers on their possessive world. This company was very closed in their thinking. Consequently, we had no effective inspection procedure at this company and had a huge management barrier to ever getting a better way proposed or deployed. This same company has the same ineffectual review procedure in place today that is really bad and is barely used. Go figure!

In another job, I had the privilege of working for a section of a very large company and had incredible support from the head person. In that environment, I was able to provide this part of the company with a slick, efficient, Web-based inspection procedure that was up to ten times faster than the existing inspection procedure. My new inspection procedure also produced higher-quality inspections and had built-in defect prevention to boot. What happened was incredible. The word spread like wildfire within my own group about how great this procedure was. That worker enthusiasm spilled over to other organizational elements that clamored to get onboard with our solution. I was deluged with training requests and guest appearances to various "all-hands" meetings regarding this way of doing things. I didn't have to do a thing to sell this. It sold itself. I knew that the software process model approach encourages better ways of doing things and encourages variances in scale or location quite naturally.

Why is the inspection procedure so critical to this software process model?

- Every activity at the "what you need to do" level has built-in inspections across the board (i.e., the inspection procedure is a how-to elaboration on all the "Inspect" verbs in all activities).
- A bad inspection procedure can have a huge detrimental effect on all activities' elapsed completion times. Conversely, an efficient inspection procedure can vastly improve activity execution times across the board.
- A good inspection procedure increases work product quality and reduces rework. Rework is expensive and should be avoided at all costs.
- A good inspection procedure gives you the basis for defect prevention — in addition to defect detection. With the software process model, you now have the ability to ask, "Where should this defect have been found?" This provides the mechanism to improve any earlier inspection checklist associated with any earlier work product. With this inspection procedure you have a built-in process-improvement mechanism in this software process model.
- Finally, an efficient inspection procedure will be used and will become part of the company culture. A bad one will not be used.

Get at Pain Issues

To be successful with process deployment, you really want to keep coming back to pain issues for any organization. The big question is, how do you do that? And how do you do it so that the data is believable? This is independent of the type of process model you're using.·

You will achieve higher levels of buy-in from all levels of the company if the perception is that you're solving real-world problems. If you separate process initiatives from "pain" issues, you will get a lot of cold shoulders about this process stuff. An absolute killer is to tie process initiatives to a maturity model (like CMMI) in a vacuum. As I mentioned before, a particular model or standard can be viewed as the flavor of the month. Some people may view all this with an "if I keep a low profile, this too shall pass" attitude. There's nothing like solving real problems — especially if people can reduce their 60-hour weeks to something more reasonable. I learned one big lesson when I got married — don't discount the power of a spouse! As Dr. Phil has said repeatedly, "If Mom's not happy, no one is happy." For most employees, you really have a shadow employee to deal with as well — the employee's spouse. If the employee can get home earlier, play with the kids more, do family things more, etc., how do you think that family unit is going to support you? Do you think you'll get early support for your next process initiative? The people part of process improvement can be enormous as a huge positive factor or a huge negative factor. The process group needs to come to grips with this aspect of deploying new processes in an organization. It is not enough to have a marvelous process framework architecture into which all the process parts fit nicely.

Personal interviews have mixed results for actually getting at pain issues. Can you be trusted as an interviewer? Will the person being interviewed be forthright or will he or she give you politically correct data? Will there be retribution if he or she dares to be totally honest? For these reasons, I would not get process problem data this way.

Two companies where I worked tried the survey route. In my opinion, surveys are best suited for getting simple check-off answers to specific questions. They are not suitable for open-ended responses. I still laugh at a British sitcom called "Yes, Prime Minister," where you can organize sets of questions and get a totally opposing poll result based on the question set — even by surveying the same people. My point here is that polls and surveys can be manipulated. Busy people tend to kick and scream about surveys and certainly want to get them off their plates as fast as possible. This means that open-ended surveys don't end up with a lot of useful data. For these reasons, surveys are not the way to go.

As an adjunct for getting at pain issues, always leave the door open for having process practitioners critique or suggest things directly or via the Web. It's a good idea to set up a "contact us" kind of Web capability so that anyone can submit issues, complaints, or recommendations directly to the process-group members. It is absolutely true that the people closest to the action are also the best ones to suggest improvements. If someone is taking the time to vent about something, it is probably important. For process people, the entire organization population is your customer. Remember that.

An Implementation Technique for Getting at Pain Issues

I have used two of the 7 M tools (modified somewhat) very successfully to get at both enterprise process pain issues and project pain issues (as a project postmortem). These two techniques have fancy names:

- Infinity brainstorming
- Interrelational digraphs

I don't use these terms when I conduct these techniques — I just call them "focus groups," "action groups," or "postmortem." Using fancy terms will turn people off. Don't do it. A focus group is fast (it usually takes less than two hours) and is totally anonymous (no retribution). This particular technique levels the playing field for quiet, introverted people versus loud, dominant people. That quiet, shy person may be the very person with a lot to express anonymously.

The most successful focus group in my experience was done with about 35 people in a single session of about an hour and a half. At this point, you're probably thinking it's impossible to have a successful session with 35 people. Conventional wisdom says the success of any meeting is conversely proportionate to the number of attendees. The higher number of people produces lower success. The lower number of people produces the higher success. This technique is just the opposite. You need at least 12 people to be successful. A small group simply won't work for this technique.

Here are the supplies needed to conduct these sessions:

- Large Post-it notes — enough for about 20 Post-its minimum per participant.
- Butcher paper or flip-chart paper — these are taped to three walls of the conference room. Four or five charts are taped to one wall. Five to six charts are taped to the opposite wall. One chart is taped on a third wall (for infinity brainstorming rules). One chart will be used to capture the major impact analysis after we collect the data

from the infinity brainstorming part of the session. The size of the room will affect how many walls are actually used. No matter what, you need two walls for charts.

■ Masking tape for the large paper sheets above.
■ Fine-point felt pens — enough for participants and facilitator.

You need a large conference room that will hold all the participants and has wall space onto which you can tape large paper charts on three walls.

Reserve this room for about two and a half to three hours to allow time for the facilitator to set up, for the actual session, and for wrapping up. The participants show up about half an hour after the room's reserved start time. At that point, all supplies should be out and the paper should be up on the walls.

This is what you need to do ahead of time:

■ Write down the session rules on a single chart. The rules are:
  – One finding per Post-it
  – You can write as many Post-its as you want within the allotted time
  – Use only the supplied fine-point felt pen for writing
  – No handwriting — print your finding
  – No names (i.e., anonymous)
  – Don't get personal — it's process related
  – Be businesslike (not crude) in your remarks
  – Make finding clear as to your intent: Can another person understand your point?
  – Be quiet when writing findings
■ Take a few minutes to explain what you will be doing to the assembled group. Make sure the group knows about your expectations and desired results. I have even put this in written form and sent it to the group ahead of time to make sure that everyone is onboard with this technique. This sets the foundation. (5 minutes maximum)
■ Announce that participants are to write one finding per Post-it note on as many Post-it notes as they want — within a ten-minute time frame. This is a totally quiet part of the technique. After writing, participants take their individual Post-its and stick them onto one wall's paper charts. Random placement is in order. This part actually creates all the pain issues as experienced by the participants in a nonretributional way because no names are used. (10 minutes maximum)

- Explain that the findings should be placed into "like" groupings by placing Post-its from one wall into Post-it groupings on another wall Like things should be clustered together; some adjustments may need to be made later. Also point out that there is a predetermined category called "orphans." (When conducting a project postmortem, I add a "good" category for the things we did right on a project.) Forget trying to establish any category names. (About 1 minute)

- Have everyone stand up, grab a pile of Post-its from one wall, and place them on another wall as Post-it clusters. Remind them that once a finding is placed, it can't be removed. Some talk among people can happen at this point. If you do this correctly, you will try to limit the category clusters to about 10–12 groups at a maximum. Have orphaned Post-its be placed under "orphans." (About 10–12 minutes)

- Identify a "reader" from the group. This individual will read the Post-its to the entire group and possibly rearrange some Post-its. (About 1-2 minutes)

- Have the reader stand up and read each Post-it finding in each cluster out loud. This accomplishes the following:
  - Everyone gets to hear all the findings.
  - Everyone gets a chance to persuade the reader to remove a Post-it if it is not in a "like" group.
  - Finally, the group establishes a mailbox name for each cluster of Post-its. Keep the name short if possible. (For project postmortems, I found that using the names from one project as predetermined names for subsequent postmortems was helpful for metrics data. However, one group disagreed with this and felt it was stifling to have a set of mostly predetermined names, especially when they disagreed with an earlier group over those names.)

- The reader repeats this for all Post-it clusters until all cluster groups have category names. During this time frame, some Post-it notes may be moved from one group to another. Finally, an attempt is made to place any and all orphaned Post-it notes into a named category. If not, they stay as orphans. This part takes the findings and attempts to categorize them for the interrelational digraph part of this technique. (15–20 minutes)

- The moderator takes a large blank matrix and writes all the category names down the left side of the matrix and then writes the same set across the top of the matrix. The moderator shades out where each category intersects with itself. You should end up with a diagonal line of shaded boxes from the top left down to the bottom right in that matrix. This is the foundation for the interrelationship digraph. We want to end up with some idea of what we need to work on first, second, third, etc., to get the biggest bang for the buck in process. (About 2 minutes)

■ The moderator reads each category name down the left side of the matrix, and asks for each, "For this category, what are the other categories that have a major impact on it?" The group participates in identifying other categories that have that major impact. The moderator simply places an "X" across the row for that targeted category. This gets repeated for each category name down the left until done. (10 minutes maximum)

■ The moderator tallies up the number of "X" marks per column and writes the totals at the bottom of each column. This provides a good idea of what categories should be attacked first that have the most impact on other things. (About 2 minutes)

■ Thank the group for their time and dismiss them.

Is this a perfect technique? No. Is it fast? Yes. Does it get at process pain issues? You bet. By spending about one and a half to two hours on this, you will extract pain issues from everybody. There is no retribution because there are no names involved. The quiet person can write stuff down anonymously just like the extroverted person can. The inputs come from the very people seeing and suffering from those pain issues.

What I have done after the session is to record all the findings by category into an Excel spreadsheet. This is a great application for counting things and coming up with percentages. This completed spreadsheet gets sent back to all the participants immediately. I have cautioned this group to keep this data under wraps because it is confidential.

The next step is to convene a senior management meeting to go over the findings and categories. The senior staff needs an understanding of what went on and that this technique gathers data rapidly. As a moderator, I take the top three categories in particular and concentrate on those for this senior management group. This is done to:

■ Acquaint the senior management on pain issues "from the trenches" and in a written form (not sanitized)

■ Identify the top three categories that, if worked, should give the biggest bang for the buck in improving or removing pain issues

■ Have this top-level management group develop an initial plan to attack the top three categories (or a subset of them)

Finally, I arrange for a feedback meeting with all the participants, so that a member of senior staff:

- Tells participants that management has heard their pain issues
- Informs participants on the plan to attack pain issues

This feedback meeting can be powerful to all involved. It closes the loop with participants and makes them feel like they have not wasted their time. It involves senior management directly with unsanitized pain issues. They can't say they didn't know about this or that. There's no place to hide. They have to do something about it. It does cause action.

When any improvements are made, you will keep going back to these pain issues. You don't tell the rank and file that you've now satisfied the first goal of some part of the CMMI! They will not relate to that at all. Tell them that these processes directly address the pain issues that were established. When regular folks get to see less pain, you will rapidly develop more and more champions to your cause. If upper management sees smoother operations, better quality, smaller time-to-market costs, better repeatability, etc., which all contribute to a healthier bottom line, you will get more champions at that level.

You can do this periodically to see how you're doing. You can do this as part of a preappraisal drill for process maturity. You can do this as a preaudit drill. The periodic approach will give you some powerful metrics related to pain issues. There's nothing like solid numbers to show your workforce that you are serious about reducing workforce pain.

Develop a Top-Level Life-Cycle Framework

This may be obvious but you really need to provide that top-level life-cycle framework into which to fit all the process pieces being developed. Without that top-level picture, there is no cohesive way of creating process elements that "fit" into anything. One vice president I worked for insisted on forming various Process Action Teams (PATs) to get some deployment items done without this in place. I was even ordered to get these groups going despite my strong objections. The results of this VP's order were absolute chaos and a huge waste of time. I sure hope none of you will deal with some of the characters I've had to endure for process development and improvement! People like that are out there. Some of them even get promoted!

Hopefully, the top-level life cycle has been developed before insertion takes place. You can do a subset top-level life cycle if your initial deployment efforts only deal with that part of the overall life cycle. For example, if you are attacking proposal-related processes, you can get away with just developing the proposal part of your life cycle. The bottom line is that you absolutely need a framework into which to fit any process elements, so that you develop once and don't need rework.

With that top-level life cycle laid out with PADs per life-cycle phase, you now have the ability to tie your pain issues to activities and to associative procedures. You also have the ability to tie event-driven procedures to any and all life-cycle phases.

Chapter 21

Deployment Issues

General Deployment Issues

Deployment problems are independent of process models. The software process model deployment has some unique challenges to overcome that I'll cover later. In general, deploying processes is the most difficult thing to do because it involves:

- Changing a company culture
- Fighting company inertia
- Fighting company politics
- Attacking sanctity of existing processes
- Overcoming possessiveness of certain individuals about any existing process basis — whether the process is working or not
- Fighting company fiefdoms
- Fighting company tribal knowledge
- Challenging people's positions

These issues manifest themselves with overt and not-so-overt back-stabbing, character assassinations, and even sabotage. I know because I have run into all this personally. You can walk into a company that is in total disarray for processes and people will fight you for trying to put in a successful process architectural model. The company can be in a death spiral and you can still experience people who will defend their turf no matter what. The politics of this can be fierce. At one company I was fired for trying to fix their major process issues. The managers viewed me as a threat to their existence. One vice president wanted a "yes man" and was horrified when I wasn't one. I had the audacity to question things and suggest improvements for the good of the enterprise.

My experience has shown that you'll have the biggest conflicts over any deployment effort with middle and upper management. Senior management is notorious for not even understanding this whole area at all. Practitioners and leads will follow process if it is simple to use and is considered helpful. The software process model certainly meets that criterion. At another place where I worked, I had top-level support and massive low-level support that collectively put the squeeze on all the middle managers from both directions. It was an awesome thing to experience personally. Those foot-dragging middle managers were beaten up from both sides. Some management holdouts were forced out over this.

In addition, the process person who questions existing situations is considered the enemy within. I have been in that very position. People have looked at me with a "who is this person" look when I dared to question the norm. You run into people that will tell you things like "that's just the way we do it here" as if that's an over-and-out statement. You will be extremely lucky if you are doing deployment in an organization that is embracing it and totally supporting your efforts.

All in all, people really fight you when you try to deploy the process model. You can be viewed as a threat to people's livelihood. The manager or director may be at that position level based on a responsibility head count. Pity the person who suggests doing things more efficiently if that level in life is threatened. I have run into whole sections that had a role once and are only there because of the "we've always done it that way" mentality. The government is notorious for this with overlapping (and opposing) agencies and responsibilities. Trade unions are also notorious for keeping the status quo — even when it makes no sense at all, such as when there were railroad union fights to keep firemen on locomotives long after steam engines went away. Once certain ways of doing things are established, it literally takes an act of Congress to remove them. The process person cannot assume that company goals for process improvement align with individual goals. There will be winners and losers. It helps to develop a thick skin as a process person because of all of this.

It is desirable to have both senior management and the process group take leadership change training. This kind of training really focuses on the change model, leadership actions needed when people are traversing the change model states, and specific tools to help that cultural change.

Deployment Issues for This Model

Remember that you need a what–how separation as a root goal. You need to mandate the "what" level while allowing flexibility and extensibility at the "how" level. I am also a big proponent that not every "what" needs a "how." Be sensible about this. Remember that success is not based on the number of process elements but on how easy it is to get to the process element of interest. Think about the Internet — you have a huge pile of potential Web pages out there but you want to get to what you want in the least amount of clicks. You want robustness behind the scenes. You want conciseness for any target Web page. An organization gets very upset if you present the process practitioners with huge scrollable lists of things. You want to head toward a very distributed Web-based solution that pays attention to process usability. Most process elements should have no (or limited) scrolling views.

These are some general things to keep in mind. The software process model brings some other aspects that you might encounter as "push back" issues:

- If piles and piles of processes are the existing base, you will encounter massive resistance to any restructuring of the existing process elements into a cohesive architecture — even when it makes sense. You may find existing "process owners" who are not about to have you mess with their "babies." It doesn't matter if their "babies" are totally useless!
- If you have process owners per part of an organization, they will resist giving up power in favor of transferring this process owner-ship to a process group.
- You will run into the "one-size-fits-all" people who do not under-stand that this model allows (and encourages) different ways of doing things. This will be a direct threat to them when alternative ways are introduced into the model.
- If Web control is vested in one part of the enterprise, you will encounter resistance to an alternative top-level life cycle–based Web page presentation versus what is there now. You will also get into power and control issues unless you have incredible senior management support.
- If you are in a paper document–oriented company, you will have a fight on your hands over the use of a single date as the version identification on your software process elements. There are people out there who are "stuck" in the '70s thinking that you have to have revision letters and numbers in order to identify any version. Stay the course on this issue.

Identify Candidate Projects

This is probably the most critical aspect of doing any kind of process deployment. When selecting candidate projects, don't ignore the people aspect involved in those projects. I mention this because at one company, the project selection was ideal; however, the people involved actually sabotaged much of the deployment efforts due to their personal biases and agendas.

Candidate projects should:

- Be at a point in the life cycle ahead of where you want to do process deployment ideally. For example, if you were addressing test-related processes, a project at the early implementation stage would be ideal.
- Have leads and managers who are process oriented and actually want success in the deployment effort.
- Be small in scope and size for deployment manageability. Don't take on huge projects as candidates if at all possible.
- Be small in number. You just need some projects as guinea pigs. Don't take on the entire enterprise for deployment.

Train Candidate Personnel

You have your candidate projects selected and you have leads and managers who are at least supportive of what you're trying to do. Now you need to make sure that affected personnel are trained in the new processes. You can't assume that they will "pick up" the new stuff. If you do, deployment will probably fail.

Training should cover:

- Overview training on the software process model approach to process
- Life-cycle training with a specific emphasis on PADs involved
- Specific procedures needed on drill-down
- Inspection procedure training in particular

Your staff might have had some of this earlier. I have found that it doesn't hurt to hit these topics again to give an edge to deployment success.

Assist Candidate Personnel

You can't just train people on these candidate projects and then say "good luck" to them. Make sure that your process-group members are geared up to assist these folks. That assistance might be:

- Embedding process people in the project during the deployment time frame
- Establishing a process "help" line
- Just-in-time training of key personnel related to process usage

Conduct Postmortem — Candidate Projects

After each candidate project "passes through" the deployment process usage time frame, take the time to conduct a postmortem with the project personnel related to the newly deployed processes.

You can use the same technique for getting at process pain issues as you do for getting postmortem results. The postmortem should be done as soon as possible after the deployment period so that everything is fresh in people's minds. You want honest inputs on what worked and what didn't work, etc. The beauty of the technique I have described is you'll get more honesty than you could ever want. As before, gather the findings, place them in a spreadsheet, and make sure the process group addresses the findings and reports back to the participants.

The result of any postmortem is some form of action. It is useless to conduct any postmortem if you're not willing to do anything about it. I mention this because a postmortem requires the process group to make necessary changes based on these inputs. It is not good enough to make process modifications. You may need to adjust training and actually retrain people related to the changes.

Rollout to Organization

After getting some real-world experience with some candidate projects, the time has come to roll out the processes throughout the entire organization. That's easier said than done. A complete rollout requires a rollout plan. Most companies have a set of projects that have different needs and are at different places in the life cycle. People involved in project maintenance may be deferred for process training if processes are developmental in nature. Some may be critical. For example, requirements management processes require new or upcoming projects to be done first. You might decide on just-in-time rollouts throughout the organization for your rollout plan. There's a lot to be said for just-in-time training because most of us forget items if we don't use them in a timely fashion.

Publicity is great during this period. Advertise what you are doing and how you plan to do it. A process-group bulletin or newsletter can be effective. All-hands sessions can also be effective related to rollout plans being disseminated to the troops.

Chapter 22

Post-Deployment Issues

Assist Organization Personnel

Just as with candidate projects, be prepared to assist people in becoming successful using any new processes. During rollout, the process group may get stretched thin doing this. I found that mobilizing candidate project personnel who are "sold" on what you are trying to do is far better than being one of those pesky "process people." You'll get a higher success rate when one practitioner can assist another practitioner.

The beauty of a rolling rollout approach is that you get more and more trainers and champions from earlier rollout projects than later ones. There's a certain amount of synergy and energy generated naturally if people are truly excited about what they are seeing and using. You will not have problems in spreading new processes throughout the organization. The reverse is also true. If the practitioners consider any process element a dog, that word will also spread.

I go back to a basic tenet that any process person needs to keep in mind — process is there to support the organization, not the other way around! Not every "what" needs a "how" procedure. Process people need to be sensible about this. I have dealt with highly technical engineering staffs who get very upset with low-level processes that they feel insult their intelligence. I have a solution here — don't do it. Leave processes at the high-level "what you have to do" steps and don't bother with any "how-to" elaboration. The software process model is flexible about this.

Collect Process Metrics

The software process model collects process metrics in a nonintrusive way via the inspection procedure and time-card association.

Because an "Inspect" step exists in all software process model activities and is done on all work products in your life cycle, you have a marvelous way of getting some real insight into the execution of this model approach. In addition, if you tie your time-card system to your software process model activities, you tie process execution to actual costs. We'll look at each for metrics collection value.

Inspection Procedure

Here's what can be derived from this procedure:

- Number of defects by activity
- Number of defects by work product
- Number of defects by life-cycle phase
- Number of defects by activity group (e.g., design, test, etc.)
- Number of defects that should have been caught earlier in the life cycle
- Cost of inspections as a quality gate
- Graph of early life-cycle defects versus testing defects
- Percentage change in inspection checklists by phase from defect prevention aspects of the inspection procedure

Time-Card Association for Actual Charges

Here's what can be derived from this connection:

- Actual costs per activity execution
- Actual costs per activity group
- Actual costs per life-cycle phase
- Actual costs of all activities related to a specific part of the system

The former provides metrics related to the targeted system. The latter provides metrics on the software process model execution itself.

Conduct Postmortems — Organization

It is vital that postmortems be conducted across the organization on the rollout processes.

The easiest way of doing this is by project, using the technique described for getting at issues (and what went right) and summarizing across these projects for an organizational perspective. For this kind of postmortem, you will find it useful to have a mostly common set of category names to compare apples to apples. I use the term "mostly" because the real world is almost never that clean. You may run into issues in one project that didn't show up in other projects.

Index

7 M (Management) Tools, xiii
    getting at pain issues with, 191–195

A

Accessibility
    to how selectors, 89
    importance to process success, 126
    integrity of, 125
Active Web storage repository, 120
Activities, 73–78
    actual costs of, 204
    aligning with project estimations, 166–167
    auditability of, 85
    as centerpiece of software process model, 86
    connection to authority level, 50
    create/update integration plan, 62
    create/update integration test, 64
    create/update unit test, 63
    criteria for, 74
    defined, 13
    design down, 61–62
    design unit/low-level design, 62
    graphical step-based format, 76–77
    implement unit, 63
    inspections built into, 71
    integrate units, 64
    as key process element, 43–48
    linking work products to, 95
    mapping to functional threads, 24
    predecessor/successor relationships to, 75
    production of work products by, 74
    on repeatable level, 50, 73
    as self-contained actions, 74
    similarities to scheduling tasks, 37
    tabular format, 76
    targeting highest instance count for process improvement, 174
    test unit, 63
    time-card charges for, 174
    training for, 110
    as verb-based items, 22
    vs. work products, 25
    as what-level process elements, 36
Activities lists, in Web implementations, 128
Activity dependencies, 79–80
Activity description, 79
Activity diagrams, xi
    activity format, 78
    graphical format, 77
    tabular format, 76
Activity drift-down, 45
Activity estimations, 84
Activity groups, 13, 57, 83
    actual costs per, 204
Activity inputs, 80
Activity metrics, 82
Activity name, 79
Activity objects, 42
Activity outputs, 82

W